T0304929

"Daniel Gros has written an easily understandable guide to self-therapy where he has effectively identified, tried, and convicted avoidance as the key culprit in maintaining pathological behavior. But more importantly, he outlines a method of recognizing, operationalizing, and confronting the four types of avoidance as a means to achieve better mental health. The book incorporates worksheets and fillable tables so the reader can set about achieving real clinical gains immediately and independently."

> —**Ron Acierno, PhD**, director of the UTHealth Trauma and Resilience Center in Houston, TX; and clinical psychologist and researcher treating post-traumatic stress disorder (PTSD) and other anxiety disorders across the lifespan

"I commend Daniel Gros for translating his many years of research developing transdiagnostic behavior therapy (TBT)—a highly effective intervention for reducing avoidance and improving quality of life for individuals suffering from a range of mental health conditions—into this practical, well-written workbook. *Overcoming Avoidance Workbook* provides a straightforward, evidence-based approach that will help you to reduce your avoidance and get your life back on track!"

> —**Randi McCabe, PhD, CPsych**, clinical psychologist, professor in the department of psychiatry and behavioral neurosciences at McMaster University, and author of *Cognitive-Behavioral Therapy in Groups*

"Wonderful! This approachable workbook targets negative emotions with state-of-the-science techniques. Daniel Gros provides an easy-to-grasp framework and practical, evidence-based steps to overcome the behaviors that feed anxiety and depression. If you are ready for change, this book is for you."

> —**Matt R. Judah, PhD**, clinical psychologist, and assistant professor of psychological science at the University of Arkansas

"Anxiety, mood, and trauma-based disorders are highly prevalent conditions that are under-treated. *Overcoming Avoidance Workbook* offers an excellent road map to overcoming such issues. Daniel Gros has distilled important science-based treatment innovations into a highly readable and clearly defined set of procedures."

—**N.B. Schmidt, PhD**, distinguished research professor, and director of the Anxiety and Behavioral Health Clinic at Florida State University

"This book guides readers straight to the heart of several of the most potent, evidence-based techniques available for anxiety and depression. Loaded with relatable examples and targeted exercises, it arms readers to battle and overcome avoidance, no matter the form it takes. It's like having a down-to-earth, no-nonsense therapist right in your hand—guiding your journey step by step and cheering you on as you work through these challenging but effective techniques."

—**Cynthia Lancaster, PhD**, assistant professor of clinical psychology at the University of Nevada, Reno

"Withdrawal and avoidance are natural responses to situations that trigger distressing emotions, though paradoxically, over-relying on these responses can increase the likelihood of experiencing these emotions over time. This book will teach you skills to reduce avoidance, cope better with unpleasant emotions, and live a more fulfilling life. It's well written, practical, easy to follow, and based on sound, evidence-based approaches. I highly recommend it!"

—**Martin M. Antony, PhD, ABPP**, professor in the department of psychology at Ryerson University, coauthor of *The Shyness and Social Anxiety Workbook*, and past president of the Association for Behavioral and Cognitive Therapies

For Alie and Henri

CONTENTS

When Avoidance Seems Like a Solution, It May Be Your Biggest Problem

IS AVOIDANCE A PROBLEM FOR YOU?

Before answering this, I want to share how I arrived at this question in the first place. I am a clinical psychologist by training, and a clinician, teacher, administrator, and researcher by trade. I have spent the last fifteen years developing these areas of my career, with the overarching goal of improving psychotherapy outcomes in my patients (through my own clinical work), in other providers' patients (through my teaching of the next generations of therapists), in the hospital systems at large (through my administrative leadership and policy development), and through innovation, investigation, and publication (through my research). It has been quite the journey, yet at times I feel like I've barely scratched the surface. However, it is this journey that led me to ask you this question and to offer you an effective way to stop avoiding and start living, through this self-help book, derived from my years of experience in these areas.

Over the years, I've been invited to speak at various universities and hospitals about my understanding of psychotherapy and how it is applied to different disorders and sets of symptoms. It is an experience that I greatly enjoy. I always begin my talks with the same slide, which starts with a common patient example: "I'm so frustrated with myself. No matter how hard I try, I cannot get myself into a grocery store. It's just too overwhelming. I have to ask my brother to pick up groceries for me." The example may sound familiar, as it is one of the more common symptoms that we see clinically. That common symptom is, of course, avoidance. I follow this patient example with the seemingly simple question: "Which disorder(s) do I have?" And while it may sound simple, I tend to get answer after answer after answer from students, faculty, and clinicians alike… "It is major depression." "It must be PTSD." "It's definitely panic disorder." "My vote is social anxiety disorder." "Don't forget about alcoholism." Or even "No way; it's irritable bowel disorder." Once the audience makes it through a lengthy list of potential diagnoses, I reveal that I don't know the answer. Because the answer could be any of the suggested diagnoses—or two or three of them. These are the most common mental health disorders, and they all have one thing in common: they all have avoidance as one of their primary symptoms.

With that start to my talk, I spend the rest of the time talking about how avoidance is the key to these disorders, and I present study after study to support my claims. (A listing of scientific articles supporting this work is provided in the Appendix.) While I promise not to bore you with scientific jargon or statistical findings in this book, you'll learn all about the negative influence that avoidance is having on the life that you want to live and how you can put an end to avoidance and start living again. In fact, all of this is very much related to the concluding slide of my talk. In that slide, I return to the same clinical example, involving the patient who needs their brother's help to buy groceries. However, I follow the example with a different question: "How do you treat my symptoms?" Unlike the flurry of differing opinions about the potential diagnosis, the answer to the treatment question is largely the same, whether I'm speaking on the East Coast of the States, the West Coast, someplace in between, or someplace beyond the border. That answer, of course, is, "You teach the patient skills to push themselves to the grocery store again and again until they learn that the experience is less negative and more positive than they had expected and they overcome their avoidance, leading to symptom improvements and recovery."

That is it. It really can be that straightforward.

You have picked up this book to find answers and start helping yourself. I am here to help. It is time for you to stop avoiding and start living.

THE TRANSDIAGNOSTIC APPROACH

There are many things that separate this book from others that you may have read when learning about your symptoms. For one, I take a "transdiagnostic" approach to presenting, understanding, and treating disorders and conditions. The term *transdiagnostic* refers to an approach that cuts across multiple disorders or sets of symptoms. For example, in contrast to other books that may focus exclusively on depression or phobias or posttraumatic stress disorder (PTSD), we will be using an approach that has been shown to address the symptoms common in each of those conditions, as well as many others (panic attacks, anger episodes, compulsions), in order to improve each disorder included in that group. The disorders or sets of symptoms covered in this text include PTSD, major depressive disorder, panic disorder, social anxiety disorder, generalized anxiety disorder, specific phobias, obsessive compulsive disorder (OCD), and many related symptoms such as impaired sleep, anger episodes, panic attacks, feeling numb or detached, and chronic worry. Just like the earlier example suggested: avoidance is a symptom that cuts across most disorders. However, you will notice that the names of these disorders and related condi-tions are not terribly important as we make our way through the exercises in each chapter. Rather, the important message is that the practices in this text can help you and your problems, whether they be one set of symptoms or four sets of symptoms; whether your symptoms have a specific name and definition or they simply are causing difficulties in your life. This approach should help—transdiagnostically.

A NOTE ON STORYTELLING

Throughout this text, I will be sharing parts of other people's stories as examples. These examples are based on patients that I have worked with over the years. Their stories are just as real as your story. And, just like your story, each of their stories started with difficult symptoms and interference in many areas in their lives. And, just as you are doing by reading this book, they decided to seek treatment for their symptoms. Over time and through some hard work, they experienced improvements in many areas of their lives, such as their social relationships, romantic relationships, education, occupation, leisure activities and interests, and community involvement. As you follow me down this same path and complete the work involved, I am confident that you will experience the same types of improvements in your life. I offer these patient stories to help guide and motivate you along the way.

HOW TO GET THE MOST OUT OF THIS BOOK

As I've said, this book was written based upon my clinical, teaching, administrative, and research experiences with psychotherapy for mental health symptoms. In particular, this book was adapted from a treatment that I have developed over the past decade: transdiagnostic behavior therapy (TBT). While treatment manuals and self-help books vary a little in their delivery, the same treatment approach underlies both. And, for both TBT and this book, the common theme is to teach readers how to identify, understand, challenge, and stop their avoidance. The book follows the exact format of TBT that has been found to be effective in hundreds of patients across multiple scientific studies. If you follow this book chapter by chapter and complete the exercises in each—especially the between-chapter practices—you should experience similar improvements in your symptoms—especially if you complete the between chapter practices. I've repeated that emphasis on purpose. As I tell my patients every session, "If you feel better for one hour a week during our session, big deal. Rather, you have to do the work in the hours between sessions to start feeling better every hour of every week." The same will be true for you as you read the chapters of this book and practice the exercises. I wrote this book to be an efficient and straightforward presentation of TBT that will be easy for readers to follow and complete on their own. However, reading a book is different from attending weekly therapy sessions in that the efficient straight-forward text presentation may go too quickly for some readers to experience the full benefits of the treatment. With that said, I encourage you to reread and repeat the exercises presented here until you feel that they have significantly reduced the symptoms that led you to read this book in the first place. I will remind you of this in the chapters as well.

In addition, if you are already working with a therapist or plan to begin, this book also can serve as an excellent companion to that treatment. TBT is growing in popularity with therapists, as shown by the studies published on it as well as the talks and trainings that I've been asked to lead (and the fact that I was asked to write this book). This book can provide an evidence-based format for your therapy sessions with the handouts and practices that are provided. Although using it with a therapist is not required for it to be successful by any means, having someone to hold you accountable and check on your progress can make a difference for those who need it (and that person could be a therapist, spouse, family member, or close friend).

Are you ready? Let's get started!

Identify the Negative Emotions and Avoidance Cycle That Hold You Back

You started this book to better understand why you aren't feeling well. Whether it be feeling sad and unmotivated about daily activities, worried and anxious about upcoming events, fearful of specific situations, or increasingly angry at just about everything that crosses your path, your negative emotions likely led you to choose this book. As you start this therapeutic journey, it's likely that these emotions feel overwhelming and unchanging. But you do not have to feel stuck like this forever. You have the power to change, to free yourself from the cycle of painful emotions and avoidance.

As we begin this week, you will be learning more about your emotions. We are going to see how opting out of life and isolating yourself is the real culprit, because of how that approach is making you feel. I hope that by learning more about yourself and your motivations, you can gain the upper hand and begin to rewrite your story. This is an important first step that we will build on over the course of the book.

Doesn't that sound easy? I didn't think so. But if you're willing to keep reading, I promise that it will work.

GETTING TO KNOW YOUR EMOTIONS

Let me begin by thanking you for giving this book a chance to work. Now, it is time to learn more about the world around you. The world that we are most concerned about is the world of your emotions; —the reason you picked up this book in the first place.

I'm going to show you a list of common emotions and symptoms found in people who, like you, experience depression, anxiety, PTSD, and stress-related conditions. While it is common for everyone to experience these symptoms from time to time, when you have these symptoms more often than not, treatment may be needed. For example, while it would be completely understandable for you to get sad after learning of a family member's death, losing a job, or ending a relationship, it is concerning when you are feeling sad more than half of the time for months at a stretch, independent of the good and bad daily news and events. You may feel as if your world always has dark clouds in the sky. The dark clouds aren't simply preceding a rainstorm or following a sunset. These dark clouds are always there.

Before we go through the list, think about these two questions and fill in your response in the space provided.

1. How much of the time do you feel negative emotions? _____ percent of the time.

2. How many days of the week do you feel sad, or angry, or nervous, or caught up in worries for no specific reason? _____ days of the week.

It's useful to give this some thought and record your sense of how much these emotions dominate your life. But whether your response was ">50 percent of the time" or "4 days a week," your negative emotions have led you to seek help through this book. The exact numbers are less important.

Common Symptoms and Negative Emotions

Circle any symptoms or emotions that you experience and feel have become concerning over time.

Depression/sadness	Checking	Guarded feeling
Low motivation	Worry	Feelings of impeding doom
Reduced energy	Anxious thoughts	Chills
Lack of drive	Headache/migraine	Hot flushes
Worthlessness	Diarrhea/urgency to go	Numb feeling
Excessive guilt	Dizziness	Choking feeling
Anxiety attacks	Obsessions	Shortness of breath
Thoughts of harming others	Compulsions	Sweating
Disrupted sleep	Irritability	Nervous tics
Increased appetite	Anger	Easily fatigued
Decreased appetite	Frustration	Restlessness
Thoughts of harming self	Yelling	Doubt
Panic	Destruction of objects	Hoarding
Upset stomach	Shyness	Flight from stressful situations
Nausea	Blushing	Nightmares
Muscle tension	Stuttering	Flashbacks
Shakiness	Avoidance of	Intrusive memories
Poor concentration	Tingling in fingers	Crying
Memory difficulties	Paleness/loss of color	Jumpiness
Racing heart rate	Light sensitivity	Feeling of unreality
Feeling of faintness	Noise sensitivity	Feeling in a daze
Fear of _____	Lack of enjoyment	Slowed movement
Pacing/agitation	Feeling of detachment	

Any other symptoms you may notice: _____

_____

Whether you circled one or many symptoms, you're here because you are experiencing too many negative emotions. There are too many dark clouds lingering. And just like clouds, negative emotions and their related symptoms tend to gather and cluster together. You may notice that you circled several similar symptoms in the list above, or that you may experience certain symptoms together in a set. These sets will become more important as you read. If you see a set of dark clouds, it typically means that a storm is brewing. The same is true for these symptoms. If your symptoms are brewing, avoidance is likely brewing too. And you can use these symptoms as a warning sign to be on the watch for avoidance and prevent the storm from getting worse.

What symptom(s) do you experience most commonly?

_____

_____

LOOKING FOR PATTERNS IN THE CLOUDS

Let's shift now to the specifics of the symptoms themselves and look for the patterns within them. When discussing negative emotions, it is common to use general terms such as depression, anxiety, and stress. However, we're going to take it a step further by describing the components that make up the symptoms, to make them easier to understand and eventually to treat.

We'll start by walking through an example together. Please think of a recent episode of particularly strong negative emotions, such as a recent anxiety attack, depressive episode, or anger incident. It may be easiest to think back to a really bad day, or a time that you received terrible news, or when you learned of an upcoming stressful event. Think of a day that the dark clouds stayed overhead all day long.

Describe your episode of strong negative emotions: _____

_____

_____

_____

Referencing the preceding list, write down the symptoms you experienced.

_____

_____

_____

_____

How did you know that you were _____? (Insert the emotion, whether depressed, anxious, worried, angry, afraid, etc.)

_____

_____

_____

_____

How were you physically feeling inside your body during that period?

_____

_____

What were you thinking about in the moment?

_____

_____

What were you doing or not doing in the moment?

_____

_____

During episodes of strong negative feelings, "subsymptoms" arise that fit into three separate categories: physical sensations, thoughts, and behaviors. As we work with your negative emotions, keep these categories in mind for your symptoms; later in the book we will be using specific treatment interventions for your physical sensations, for your thoughts, and for your behaviors (or more likely lack of behaviors). In fact, it is the lack of behaviors that will be highlighted again and again, going by names such as *avoidance*, *withdrawal*, and *isolation*. For now, it is important to think of those symptoms as the villains of your story.

Speaking of stories: as mentioned in the introduction, I will be sharing parts of other people's stories as examples throughout this text. Their stories are just as real as your story—and hopefully, through their challenges and victories, offer you a chance to reevaluate your own experience. And, just like your story, their stories had to start at the beginning too. Let's start by learning about the stories of Andrew and of Susan.

Andrew's Story: Panic, Fear, and Anxiety

Andrew always has been a nervous guy, ever since he was a little kid. He never liked to be the center of attention and would pretend to be sick whenever he had a presentation to do in school. And that didn't change for Andrew when he grew up. However now, he had more control over what he wants to do and not to do—most of the time, that is. Despite picking a job that he can work on from home, and spending time only with his small group of friends at one friend's place or another, he cannot avoid all social gatherings. The day has come that his little brother, Steven, is getting married. Andrew has been a nervous wreck leading up to the day. All that he can think about is the crowd of people and being forced into conversations. And his brother even asked him to be his best man and give a toast at the reception.

It's now the morning before the wedding. He knows that he has to go, and his anxiety is mounting and mounting, to the point where Andrew experiences a panic attack while he's getting ready to leave. If Andrew were to deconstruct his anxious feelings into physical sensations, thoughts, and behaviors, it might look something like this:

Physical	Thoughts	Behaviors
Racing heart	I'm going to die	Pacing
Rapid breathing	I'm going crazy	Wringing hands
Dizziness	I have to get out of here	Plotting how to escape the situation (considering ways to leave the wedding early)
Muscle tension	It is not safe	Avoiding (considering ways to skip the wedding altogether)
Sweating		
Tingling in fingers		
Upset stomach		
Shakiness		

Susan's Story: Depression

Susan thought that she had the perfect life. She had the marketing job that she had always wanted. She had married her college sweetheart. And they had just moved into the perfect house in a great neighborhood. Everything was going well, until it wasn't. Susan found herself bickering with her husband all of the time, dreading the morning commute to work and falling behind in her work assignments, and spending more and more time watching television alone in her bedroom. She was finding reasons not to go out with friends or return calls from family members. Over time, her husband gave up and moved out, and even her friends stopped trying to reach her after their calls went straight to voicemail over and over. Although this bothers her at times, she just wants to be left alone. If Susan were to break down her feelings into physical sensations, thoughts, and behaviors, it might look something like this:

Physical	Thoughts	Behaviors
Slowing heart rate	It's not worth it	Lying in bed longer than she intended
Slowed breathing	Nothing is going to change	Showing up late to work or finding reasons to escape/leave early
Feeling of heaviness	It's just too hard	Skipping/avoiding obligations
Fatigue		

CATEGORIZING YOUR SYMPTOMS

Now it's your turn. Let's return to the really bad day, or a time that you received terrible news or learned of an upcoming stressful event that you identified previously. Think through that situation and list your symptoms in the three categories of physical sensations, thoughts, and behaviors, just as Andrew and Susan did.

Primary Negative Emotion: _____

Physical	Thoughts	Behaviors

Looking at your entries in the table, what do you notice about your symptoms? _____

_____

_____

What were the most common behaviors that you noticed? _____

_____

WHEN THE DARK CLOUDS TURN INTO A HURRICANE (OR JUST ANOTHER RAINSTORM)

Now we're on the same page. We've set your story based on specific patterns of negative emotions that keep happening, and we've talked about how to find the patterns in your symptom in terms of their associated physical sensations, thoughts, and behaviors (or lack of behaviors). However, before moving on, we need to address a couple of severe symptom reactions that may arise at times. Although these symptoms are less common than other symptoms that we have covered so far, they can be quite serious when they arise, so it's important to recognize them. You may or may not have experienced these types of severe symptoms, but I want you to know about them and how to manage them should they occur. Put another way, while not all storms are severe, you need to have a plan for when a storm turns into a hurricane and heads your way. These severe symptoms are first, panic and anxiety attacks, and second, suicidal and homicidal thoughts.

Panic or Anxiety Attacks (the storm that turns out to be just rain)

The negative emotional experience called a panic attack is associated with a strong physical reaction. We touched on it briefly in Andrew's story. Most people have experienced at least one panic attack, typically during a period of intense stress. Andrew's list of physical sensations included racing heart, rapid breathing, dizziness, muscle tension, sweating, tingling or numbness in his fingers, upset stomach, and shakiness.

As a set, these physical sensations can cause fear and anxiety in and of themselves and sometimes even drive the person to seek emergency care. For example, if Andrew had walked into a hospital with a rapid heart rate and breathing, dizziness, shaking, and sweating, the hospital staff would likely call for a gurney and bring him to the emergency room for testing. However, are these physical symptoms actually dangerous? Can they lead to a heart attack? Can they cause someone to go crazy or lose control?"

Well, the simple answer is no. Absent any underlying health conditions (heart disease, impaired lung function), they can't cause any of those things. Here is why. Have you ever heard of the fight-or-flight response? It's the body's natural defense mechanism, shared throughout the animal kingdom. The body essentially shifts into autopilot to either prepare to fight off danger or run away. Every body system shifts to protect you from the (perceived) danger.

- Your *heart* races to circulate blood to your vital organs (lungs) and arms and legs.

- Your *breathing* accelerates to get the oxygen needed to fight or run.

- Your muscles *tense*; in fact, they tense so much that your hands begin to *shake* and your blood pressure may rise, causing slight *dizziness*. .

- You experience *butterflies in your stomach*, along with *dry mouth* and *tingling* in your fingers, as your body starts to shut off nonessential systems (digestion), and moves your blood away from nonessential areas (fingers, nose, toes).

This fight-or-flight response, or panic attack, is designed to keep you alive; therefore it *cannot* and *will not* hurt you. There are some extreme exceptions to this rule; namely, if your heart and lungs are not healthy enough to support your climbing a few flights of stairs, you are not healthy enough to weather a panic attack and should seek medical care. However, as long as you are in even slightly good physical shape, panic attacks are not physically dangerous to you and there's no need for urgent or emergent interventions.

In the course of this treatment, you will learn how to push through these attacks if you experience them. They are a natural response to intense stress, anxiety, and fear (or even anger), and learning how to work through them is a critical step in your getting better. And so, in the case of panic attacks, while the pattern of dark clouds may feel like an approaching hurricane, it ends up being a harmless storm that releases a downpour and then clears on its own. While unpleasant, it poses no danger. You just let it pass and resume your activity, or pay it no attention and keep going, rain or shine.

Note: if you are concerned about the specific physical symptoms, please consult with a physician.

Episodes Involving Suicidal and Homicidal Thoughts (the hurricane that must be prepared for, with action taken when needed)

Another serious symptom associated with the negative emotions are that of suicidal and homicidal thoughts. These thoughts tend to be most associated with severe depression but can be experienced by anyone and in any situation. They can come on suddenly in response to stress or develop slowly over weeks, months, or even years of experiencing untreated symptoms. Unlike panic attacks or other seemingly urgent, but nonthreatening symptoms, suicidal and homicidal thoughts *should be reported immediately* to a health care professional.

If you or someone you know may be considering suicide or homicide, in the United States, you can contact the National Suicide Prevention Lifeline (https://suicidepreventionlifeline.org/) at 1-800-273-8255 (En Español: 1-888-628-9454; Deaf and Hard of Hearing: 1-800-799-4889) or the Crisis Text Line (https://www.crisistextline.org/) by texting 741741. Or, if it is a true emergency with a life in imminent danger, call 911 or report to your local emergency room.

For readers in countries outside of the United States, contact your local emergency services or report to the nearest hospital with emergency services. Unlike the comparison of a panic attack to a harmless rainstorm, suicidal and homicidal thoughts should be likened to a dangerous hurricane. However, just like a hurricane, you can learn to notice the warning signs, and you should always have a plan in place for seeking immediate help to manage the approaching storm. Like panic attacks, the storm of suicidal and homicidal thoughts will pass with time too. The storm will come (or miss you altogether) and go, and you will ready to get back to life's challenges and satisfactions, better prepared for the next storm (if one comes).

THE IMPORTANCE OF AVOIDANCE

I hope that now you have gained better recognition of your negative emotions and know some simple strategies to use when these emotional storms get too intense. Developing these skills is like finding patterns in the clouds. The patterns when you experience negative emotions are: (1) physical sensations, such as heart racing, rapid breathing, and fatigue; (2) thoughts, such as *I'm going crazy* or *I just want to be left alone*; and (3) behaviors, such as avoiding a crowded party or staying in bed all day. If you need a reminder, look back at the "Categorizing Your Symptoms" table you filled in earlier, or make a copy of the blank table to use if different emotional experiences arise.

Now that you have a new perspective on your symptoms, we are going to take another step forward in understanding the key to your story: identifying and reversing avoidance, withdrawal, and isolation. These are the main obstacles on your journey back into a living a full life. As we will discuss, they may not feel much like villains right now. They may even seem like the friends that you rely on to "help" you manage your strong negative emotions. However, we are about to learn that they are only making things worse and causing more dark clouds overhead. Let's start by understanding what avoidance is, how it makes matters worse, and how to start on your journey toward healing by tackling avoidance head on.

GETTING TO KNOW YOUR AVOIDANCE

Whether you are aware of it or not, avoidance plays a major role in your life, and it has for some time. In some cases, it was probably for the best. As a child, you were told "Don't talk to strangers" or "Don't swim 30 minutes after eating" or "Don't eat food that fell on the floor." In other cases, it may have been less clear, such as "Don't step on a crack or you'll break your mother's back," "Boys don't cry" or "Stop being such a girl." You've probably heard most of these sayings throughout your life, whether from your parents, friends, and teachers, or on television or online media. Each of these is an example of how we are taught to avoid.

However, these instructions to avoid did not stop in childhood. As an adult, you have heard "Avoid the highway traffic at rush hour," "Avoid being out in the sun for prolonged periods without sunblock," and "Avoid eating too many carbs." Again, while some of these recommendations may be helpful, others may be less so. Still others can be taken to another level—a harmful one—due to life circumstances and stressors and the way we are affected by our negative emotions.

If you are reading this book, it is likely that this last sentence rings true for you. The combination of avoidance and negative emotions has become a major issue in your life. It is likely that because of how you are feeling, you have avoided talking to family members, or avoided spending time with friends, or even perhaps avoided seeking help until now. And, as we will see, avoiding situations only makes your emotions worse. Let's start this deep dive into avoidance by taking an honest look at your behavior.

SEEING YOURSELF THROUGH A VIDEO CAMERA

This is a great exercise for seeing the influence of avoidance on your life. Imagine that someone is following you around with a video camera for a week. Imagine that it is an older camera, so it can't zoom in on facial expressions or record your conversations. The camera can only see what you are doing.

Describe what it would see you doing last Monday night.

_____

_____

_____

_____

Describe what the video camera would see you doing last Tuesday morning.

_____

_____

_____

_____

Describe what it would see you doing last Friday night. _____

_____

_____

_____

Now let's try another step. How could the camera tell that you're experiencing negative emotions?

_____

_____

_____

_____

- Someone with depression might observe, "I see myself just shifting from my bed to my couch to my bed day after day."

- A person with anxiety commonly says, "I see myself getting so caught up in my worries that I forget about important events or just skip them altogether."

- A person with panic attacks commonly says, "It looks like I rarely leave the house, and I make my spouse do everything for me."

- A person with anger may say, "I see myself trying to avoid frustrations by rushing myself through interactions or staying away from them altogether."

In each of these examples (as is probably the case for your description), avoidance plays a key role in negative emotions. The power of this example is that it highlights the connection between what you're doing (or not doing) and your negative emotions. It shows how much influence avoidance and isolation may be playing in your life.

Mark's Story

Several years ago, I worked with Mark, a thirty-six-year-old man who lived in Western New York. I asked Mark to do this video camera exercise. Although he was skeptical, Mark trusted me and the potential benefits from treatment that I was describing, so he obliged me. When he returned the next week, Mark shared his shock at how boring and sad his life looked from the outside.

It had taken Mark years to realize that he spent hours upon hours inside his home, sitting in front of his television or phone or using his television and phone simultaneously. Sure, Mark went to work when he felt up to it and did what he needed to do when he absolutely had to do it, such as waiting for the final day (or the day after that) to pay his bills, or making an appointment at the auto repair shop (when his car was making ominous clunking sounds or had actually stalled out on the driveway), but through that video camera he could see he was doing little to nothing else. He sat on the couch. He flipped channels. Sometimes he napped without intending to; other times he might start a quick task or chore without finishing it, such as cleaning just enough dishes to use for his next meal (before he switched to paper plates to avoid the whole ordeal of dishwashing) or doing a mixed load of laundry without remembering to move it to the dryer (and then relying on the "smell test" to identify the dirty laundry that was still tolerable to wear). And, of course, the hypothetical camera showed Mark getting one beer, one more beer, or maybe several more, leading to another unintended nap. He also realized that there should have been more in his life. The camera should have showed him at his nephew's little league game on Saturday or at his buddy's fantasy football draft on Sunday. But, he never made it out that weekend. Maybe he wasn't feeling well or drank too many beers to leave the house. The camera couldn't show those reasons or excuses (or the negative emotions that Mark was experiencing inside); it only showed him staying home for yet another weekend.

HOW AVOIDANCE IS INFLUENCING YOUR WORLD

For Mark, and for you, it is crucial to see yourself honestly. The distress that you are feeling is real and strong. But as your avoidance of activities that cause you distress keeps you at home or away from things that are important to you, it also is moving you further and further away from life. At this point in your story, avoidance, isolation, and withdrawal are winning—and you are losing.

Now that you've completed the Seeing Yourself Through a Video Camera exercise and gotten your first clear view of your avoidance and negative emotions, let's walk through the way psychologists like me think about negative emotions and avoidance to better understand the connection between the two.

The process begins with an initial event or series of events leading someone to experience negative emotions, such as fear, anxiety, anger, or depression. This event could be fifty different things causing initial negative emotions for fifty different people, or fifty different things all giving one person negative emotions. Examples include losing one's job, separating from a spouse, death of a loved one, having an unexpected panic attack, witnessing or experiencing a traumatic event—the possibilities are endless. It could be one very big thing or a bunch of smaller things. Yours is unique to you, Mark's is unique to him, and it is likely what led you to pick up this book.

Whatever the case, it started the cycle of avoidance for you. However, the problem is not the initial negative emotions associated with the event(s). It is normal to feel badly when bad things happen. Negative emotions are not the real villain; rather, it is when the person chooses avoidance and isolation to *cope* with the negative emotions that bigger problems are likely to arise. Essentially, the person is taking a step back from the world around them, including both the stressful things (difficulty with paying bills after job loss) and potentially healthy things (support from family members after losing a loved one) in their life. The more someone pulls away, the worse they feel; and, the worse they feel, the more they want to pull away. This is when avoidance takes over. In fact, over time the avoidance and negative emotions eventually become so severe that although the initial event or reason for the initial avoidance may have become a little unclear (perhaps you've gotten over the breakup with your boyfriend), the cycle of negative emotions and avoidance continues, each reinforcing the other (so you don't start dating again, you avoid friends with or without significant relationships, and you don't bother going downtown any more, all leading to increased depression and loneliness).

Figure 1.1 depicts what this looks like.

Figure 1.1. Model for Negative Emotions (Anxiety, Fear, and Depression)

The cycle typically begins with a negative event or series of negative events leading to negative emotions, which in turn cause an individual to pull back from the world around them.

Although it may feel like it's helpful to just relax, sleep in, or avoid stress, the reality is that the isolation, withdrawal, and avoidance make the negative emotions get worse.

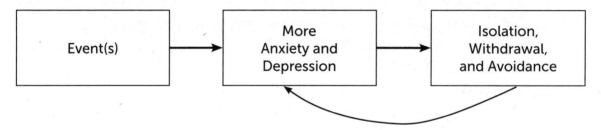

The more negative emotions you experience, the stronger the urge will be to isolate and avoid.

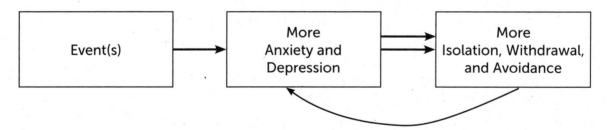

And of course, the more you isolate and avoid, the worse you feel, until the cycle takes on a life of its own. Even if the event(s) that started it all fades, the pattern of isolation and avoidance maintains the negative emotions.

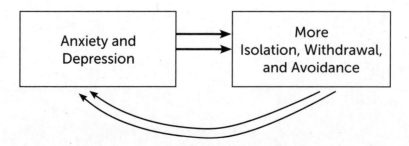

Mark's Story (continued)

Let's look back at Mark and see how the model fits his experience. Mark wasn't always feeling stuck and depressed, missing out on the things that he values. If we rewind his story, Mark was married, working his way up in his company, and spending his free time with family and friends. However, the mounting financial pressures resulted from some poor decisions (buying a used car from a friend that ultimately broke down, buying too many lottery tickets during a large jackpot, spending too much money and time at the bar) and the frequent arguments that followed took a toll on Mark's marriage. Mark and his wife pulled further away from each other, and their negative feelings toward each other mounted along the way.

Eventually, Mark's wife had had enough, and she moved out. Mark came home from work to a half-empty home. This stunning turn of events was very difficult for Mark. He began to feel depressed; he started avoiding activities he had previously enjoyed. He was now living alone, missing the previous interactions and shared activities with his wife. Mark began to withdraw from work as well, by calling in sick with increasing frequency, noting that he didn't feel up to being around his coworkers and hearing about their happy marriages. Mark also avoided time with friends and family, because he knew they would ask him how he was doing or want to talk about his wife's leaving. Over time, his initial avoidance triggered by the event and associated depression turned into a downward spiral. His boss at work started complaining about Mark's frequent absences, and Mark felt guilt and shame at this situation (increased negative emotions); rather than face the problem and address it, Mark eventually quit his job (increased avoidance). Mark's friends, who at first tried to be there for him and offer him support, got frustrated and lost hope after their calls and texts kept going unanswered. Mark would simply let the alerts pile up on his phone, feeling paralyzed by his shame over his lost relationships (increased negative emotions) and never bothering to even listen to the voicemails (increased avoidance). Over time, his friends simply lost touch with Mark. And Mark's calls with his extended family became shorter and less frequent and his visits were fewer and farther between. Years after the original crisis, despite mostly getting over his divorce and finding a new job (one that was far less demanding and did not pay as well), Mark remained depressed and largely isolated, spending his afternoons and weekends alone drinking one beer after another.

Given this example, can you think of any events, such as those leading to Mark's negative emotions and avoidance, that may have contributed to your own initial avoidance, withdrawal, or isolation? List them here.

Possible events/contributors to avoidance: _____

_____

_____

_____

_____

Again, depending on the duration of your symptoms (months, years, decades), you may not be able to connect the onset of your negative emotions to a specific event. Fortunately, you don't have to identify a specific cause in order to treat your negative emotions and avoidance, although it may be helpful to understanding the original source.

HOW AVOIDANCE LEADS YOU DOWN THE WRONG PATH

Avoidance and isolation are natural reactions to negative emotions, such as depression, anxiety, fear, and anger. It was a natural response for Mark and countless others. But why? Why do we turn to avoidance to cope with our negative emotions? Well, although avoidance is associated with a lot of negatives, we can certainly generate positive feelings through avoidance and isolation.

Put simply, sometimes it may *feel better* to avoid.

Think about the ordinary avoidance choices that we all make from time to time. Would you rather battle rush hour and face a tough day at work—or call in sick, stay under the covers, and sleep in? Would we rather fight the crowds at a popular restaurant or grab takeout and eat in front of the television at home?

Can you think of ways that you've used avoidance in seemingly positive ways (avoiding a difficult assignment)? Please list a few below.

_____

_____

_____

_____

However, these positive feelings typically are mild and limited. Sure, you might gain a reduction in discomfort. Mark's fourth beer every night may have made him feel a little better...in the short term (and with a hangover in the morning). But of course, there's always a downside to the avoidance. The short-term benefits of avoiding and isolating frequently lead to problems, and in the long term they prevent finding a real solution. But the short-term comfort and relief is how your avoidance tricks you into following the path into a darker place (negative emotions). Let's look at a few examples before we explore yours.

Avoidance	Short-term (positive) results	Long-term (negative) results	Longer-term results
Stayed in bed and slept in all morning, rather than starting a difficult task at work (depression).	It feels better to sleep in than struggle through a difficult task.	The task goes unfinished, and as time passes, new tasks are added.	The more the tasks are avoided, the more difficult it becomes to manage the pile. This leads to a poorer work evaluation.
Skipped a Mother's Day dinner with the family, rather than facing the crowded restaurant (fear).	Avoids the uncomfortable, distressing feelings of being caught in a crowd.	The dinner is missed, and the family is disappointed.	The more crowds are avoided, the more difficult it becomes to be in crowds in the future. Over time, this will strain family and friend relationships, who feel they can't rely on the person.

Avoidance	Short-term (positive) results	Long-term (negative) results	Longer-term results
Checked an assignment over and over, rather than turning it in to the professor and moving on to the next one (anxiety).	Anxiety is reduced, as every item has been quadruple-checked.	Checking is time consuming and leaves less time available to complete a task, even with a single check.	The next assignment is due before the first is finished. This will hurt the grade of all the papers, and soon the person will become overwhelmed.
Refusing to talk to a neighbor because "they wronged you" in a recent interaction (anger).	Staying away prevents the further buildup of anger.	A temporary time-out turns into long-term avoidance and a broken relationship.	The once-healthy friendship is replaced by unending efforts to ignore or avoid the neighbor, leaving others (e.g., their spouse talking to the neighbor's spouse) to try to make excuses for their behaviors.

Let's review that previous question again. Can you think of ways that you've used avoidance in seemingly positive ways (avoiding a difficult assignment) that resulted in a long-term negative result (getting fired from work)? List a few of these.

_____

_____

_____

_____

_____

_____

Over the coming weeks, we are going to spend a lot of time helping you to work through the habit of short-term positive avoidance in order to reverse the long-term negatives that you've experienced. The tricky thing about avoidance is that it often comes with immediate short-term positives, but over time it ultimately traps you. We will find a way to see through this trickery together. It will take a little while to get there, but starting to realize why you are avoiding is an important step in this process.

KEEPING TABS

You've learned how avoidance develops and is maintained and how it contributes to the worsening of negative emotions in your life. Over the coming weeks, you will learn strategies to overcome your avoidance and begin to feel better—to stop avoiding and start living. But first, as part of that process, you'll want to become more aware of how you use avoidance in your daily life.

- *When* are you using avoidance?

- *Where* are you using avoidance?

- *How* are you using avoidance?

I would like you to start keeping an eye out for avoidance in your life and use the form provided here to begin tracking it. You're going to get to know where and when avoidance is causing trouble in your world and driving your negative emotions (or your lack of positive emotions). Use the Record of Avoided Situations Worksheet to list any instances of avoidance that you either already know about or notice in the coming days and weeks, along with your associated emotions. In some cases, your avoidance may be associated with a strong negative emotion (sadness, anxiety, fear); other times it may be associated with a lack of positive emotion (disinterest, numbing, lack of motivation). Although it may take time for you to start noticing, you will be surprised by the amount of avoidance that you will be able to list. Additional copies of this form can be printed from http://www.newharbinger.com/45663.

Record of Avoided Situations Worksheet

Using the space provided, record any person, place, thing, task, activity, thought, or memory that you have avoided or had to depart from earlier than you originally planned, because of either your negative emotions (depression, anxiety, fear) or the absence of positive emotions (disinterest, lack of motivation). These might include shopping at certain stores, driving on certain roads, eating at certain restaurants, visiting certain public places, thinking or talking about certain past events, or completing certain tasks/activities. Include examples from your present and recent past. Ratings could be negative emotions (–100 to 0) or lack of positive emotions (0 to +100), with –100 as the most severe negative emotions, 0 as completely neutral, and +100 as the most positive emotions. I've filled in examples to get you started.

Person/Place/Thing/Task/Activity/Thought/Memory	Emotion	Rating (–100 to +100)
Shopping at busy grocery store	fear	–75
Going to kid's soccer game	disinterest	10

Person/Place/Thing/Task/Activity/Thought/ Memory	Emotion	Rating (−100 to +100)

Becoming aware of when you avoid is the most crucial step toward taking your life back. The hope, and goal of this book, is that as you continue to track the times when you are running from life, it will become easier both to identify these situations and to challenge yourself and put the avoidance response behind you. And as avoidance weakens and you start to feel better over time, your records in each chapter's form will get shorter and shorter.

We are on this journey together; we will get you there. Avoidance doesn't stand a chance.

WRAPPING UP

I hope you are now beginning to see that although these emotions are powerful, they can be broken down into pieces that both are easier to understand and eventually will become easier to treat. The more time that you spend investigating your dark clouds, the easier it will become to notice the patterns (as well as the warning signs for a storm). When you experience your next episode of symptoms, please think about them in the categories that we discussed (physical sensations, thoughts, and behaviors), focusing on the certain behaviors (avoidance) that you are using to try to cope, and how (in)effective they are.

Remember, it is what you *do* that really matters and affects how you are feeling. It is what you are *not doing* that is getting you into trouble. The cycle of negative feelings and *not doing* (avoidance and isolation) is the heart of the problem. Whether it is due to your trying to cope with difficult feelings or with damaging events, it is your walking away from places, behaviors, and people that is making everything worse. Although it may bring temporary relief, it ultimately feeds the exact emotions you are hoping to prevent. Just like a household pest or Hollywood monster, the more your avoidance feeds your negative feelings (and lack of positive feelings), the bigger your problems will grow.

For this coming week, I want you to take notice of your avoidance and enter them in the Record of Avoided Situations Worksheet. Where is avoidance happening for you, and how often? How is avoidance interfering with the life that you want? The first step of fixing any problem is to understand it.

In the next chapter, we will identify your treatment goals and lock in your reasons to start making the changes that you need to make to recover from your negative emotions. Once you have completed that step, you will be ready to go ahead and stop avoiding and start living.

Set Your Treatment Goals and Gather Your Motivations for Change

Over the last week, you have been learning how avoidance and isolation are the key to the problems that you've been experiencing. Your negative emotions (or lack of positive emotions) and avoidance feed on each other following a stressful or even traumatic event. Yes, sometimes it feels better to simply stay home rather go to the crowded gathering, to avoid your boss rather than face up to your team's mistake at work, or to turn the alarm off and go back to sleep rather than drag yourself out of bed and face your daily stressors. But as you have been tracking your feelings and behaviors, you've realized that it is these short-term benefits of avoidance and isolation that keep the cycle going.

However, you also learned that the short-term benefits of avoidance and isolation are tied to long-term negatives. For example, repeatedly staying home and away from crowds can make even the shortest line at your favorite fast-food restaurant yet another excuse to go back home without buying your meal. Or repeatedly avoiding your boss and skipping meetings can lead to being written up at work and eventual job loss (or a good excuse to quit and just stay home; Mark did just that in the previous chapter).

As you have been tracking your avoidance to see when, where, and how you were using it throughout your weekly schedule, you've gained a new perspective on your emotions. You've seen the role played by avoidance. You know what you need to overcome. You know what must be defeated for you—well, if not to live that illusory fairytale "happily ever after," at least to experience fewer negative emotions and replace them with plenty of positive experiences and feelings.

This week, I'll ask you to think about what you want to accomplish with this book. This means becoming better acquainted with the potential hero of your story: namely *you*. I will push you to set goals to become that hero.

And there cannot be a hero without an adventure. We will be building your story by identifying the *whys*. More specifically, why did you pick up this book? Why have you begun reading the chapters and attempting the exercises? Why are you motivated to try to stop avoiding and start living?

HOW ARE YOU AVOIDING?

Obviously, we have big ideas for this chapter. We are talking about becoming heroes and planning a victorious adventure. But before we get to that, we need to review your homework, the Record of Avoided Situations Worksheet in week 1. There wouldn't be much use in assigning a task without reviewing it with you and asking you some follow-up questions. We need to look honestly at the week just past, or however how much time has passed since you completed the last chapter. Granted, this record is not a static document— it should continue to change over time. In fact, you should notice more and more situations or events that you are avoiding and may well be shocked by the extent of it. But as treatment gets going, you should begin to cross out more and more situations that you are *no longer* avoiding as you work through the treatment and start living more fully—and having a lot more fun along the way.

Okay. Let's start by revisiting your Record of Avoided Situations Worksheet and asking some questions. Circle your answers.

Were you able to identify things that you were avoiding?   Yes   No

For most people, these may be difficult to identify at first. Once you find a few, they will begin to flow until the list begins to fill. For example, if you avoid one restaurant or one store, are there similar places that you are avoiding too (movie theater, bars, sporting events, festivals)? If you continue to struggle to identify situations you avoid, you may want to reread the previous chapter, or try asking a friend, family member, or neighbor what they think. If you don't have a person to ask, is that due to your avoidance and isolation? Perhaps the answer can help you identify something you're avoiding.

Do you see any patterns in the types of things that you avoid?

Avoidance tends to cluster. Do you have more avoided activities in which you are alone (going to the movies alone) or those that put you in a crowd (going to a popular bar)?

              Alone   Crowd

Is your avoidance more associated with feeling…

| Down | Anxious | Angry | Afraid | Just not feeling at all (no energy, motivation, enjoyment) |

We will spend more time on categorizing your avoidance later in the book. For now, just keep digging in the areas where you find some avoidance. For example, do you avoid only lines at banks, or do you also tend to avoid long lines at grocery stores, restaurants, restrooms, and the like?

Write down any other patterns you notice: _____

_____

_____

We will revisit these lists again and again as we move through the chapters. You'll be keeping close tabs on the villain (avoidance) in your story. Please keep recording and looking for patterns (to find more avoidance to track).

IDENTIFYING YOUR GOALS

As is true any time you're learning something new, goal setting is an essential part of your treatment, to identify what you are working toward. In many situations, goals may be obvious to you. If you're building a fence around the backyard, you're done when the last rail is attached. If you're changing your car battery, you're done when you turn the key in the ignition and the engine turns over. If you trying to rescue a princess, you're done when you've successfully stormed the castle and freed her from the danger. However, when it comes to your depression and anxiety and other negative emotions, the goals can be harder to know. For example, how will you know that treatment of your depression is successful? How will you know when treatment of your anxiety has been effective?

You may be thinking *I just want to feel better* or *I want to be normal again.* The trouble with these types of goals are it can be hard to measure them and tell when you have accomplished what you aimed for. What does feeling better actually mean? What is normal? There is no blood test to tell you that your anger levels are within "normal" range, nor is there a scale that you can stand on weekly to tell you that your fear of driving has gone from constraining your mobility to a feeling of freedom and relaxed confidence.

So let's return to the example from the previous chapter and apply it to your goals.

If someone followed you around with a video camera, how would they know that you have difficulties with depression, anxiety, or stress?

_____

_____

_____

Taking it a step further, if they continued to follow you around with a video camera during treatment, how would they know that you've *overcome* your difficulties with depression, anxiety, or stress?

_____

_____

_____

Take a moment to review the following example. Observe how a troubling feeling or symptom (anger) was made into a general goal (feeling less angry) and then into an observable or testable goal (being able to stand in line at the grocery store without leaving).

(Example) Treatment Goals

Goal #1:   <u>Feeling less angry and short—tempered around strangers</u>

How is avoidance/isolation involved: <u>Avoiding people that I don't know and can't trust</u>

Observable/measurable change (how would others see the change):   <u>Standing in line at grocery store without leaving; eating with family in restaurant without taking breaks outside or leaving early; attending work holiday party with my wife and making small talk</u>

Now it's your turn. Can you think of similar goals for yourself? Are there measurable ways to show through that camera lens that you've improved?

Before you do, I know you may find this to be one of the more difficult tasks. This is common in the beginning. It is common to feel that these symptoms are unchangeable or simply part of who you are now (or even beneficial in some cases). Again, avoidance has many tricks. And, while some of that may be true right now, it doesn't have to stay that way. Whether it's been four months, four years, or even four decades since your symptoms began to take hold, they remain just symptoms of a treatable problem. Once you have targeted them, you can make changes and stop avoiding and start living.

Realize, too, that your goals will not be set in stone. You should expect to further clarify and expand these goals, as well as add new goals as you have reached and better understood your original targets. Let's use physical exercise as an example. When you first start working out, your goals might be big (running a marathon) or small (walking a mile). However, as you reach certain milestones, these goals may need to be specified and adjusted over time (running in the local 10k race). You will treat your symptom goals in the same manner, and revisit them in future chapters. Again, if you are going to be the hero of this story and succeed in treatment, you need to know where to start and what to target. Try to go through at least three symptoms and create observable goals to target each on the form provided. Additional copies of this form can be printed from http://www.newharbinger.com/45663.

Treatment Goals

Goal #1: _____

How avoidance/isolation is involved: _____

Observable/measurable change (how others would see the change): _____

_____

_____

Goal #2: _____

How avoidance/isolation is involved: _____

Observable/measurable change (how others would see the change): _____

_____

_____

Goal #3: _____

How avoidance/isolation is involved: _____

Observable/measurable change (how others would see the change): _____

_____

_____

Goal #4: _____

How avoidance/isolation is involved: _____

Observable/measurable change (how others would see the change): _____

_____

_____

Goal #5: _____

How avoidance/isolation is involved: _____

Observable/measurable change (how others would see the change): _____

_____

_____

This is optional, but you may find it helpful to both identify these targets on your own as well as share the experience with someone close to you. Whether it be your spouse, your parent, or a close friend, this person can sometimes provide another view of what is going on and what could change. Essentially, they offer that outside view or camera that can already see how avoidance and isolation and their related emotions are interfering with the life that you want to live. They may be able to see what you cannot, and you should use that to your advantage when it comes to finding things to change.

JUSTIFY CHANGE

Now that you've set your initial goals, you need to identify the reasons for making your changes. This treatment process is not going to be easy. If it were, you would have already completed it and wouldn't have picked up this book. And so, you need to develop tools to help you push through the challenges ahead. Just as in the earlier example, the hero of the story needs to know *why* they fight. You need to know your *whys* too. Begin considering why you are deciding to make these changes now. What's the point in going through this? It might get hard, but it won't get too hard if you have your *why*.

You've been through tough times before—whether it was making it through the final weeks of school; recovering from an injury, illness, or surgery; or overcoming significant financial difficulties. In each of these scenarios, you always had an opportunity to simply give up. However, you found a way through them, likely by focusing on what is most important to you. Rather than waiting until you're faced with challenges and the opportunity to push forward (or give up), it helps to understand your reasons from the start so you can push through when it matters.

Here are some common examples that you might identify with.

(Example) Reasons for Making Change Worksheet

Reason #1:   To be there for my family (wife and daughter)

Reason #2:   To return to work (or school) and support my family again

Reason #3:   To make my dad/mom proud of me again

Reason #4:   To stop missing out on activities with friends/family

Reason #5:   To get healthy

Now it's your turn to lock in reasons for making changes. Similar to your treatment goals, you will be asked to revisit these reasons over time and update them as needed. Additional copies of this form can be printed from http://www.newharbinger.com/45663. Please feel free to borrow from any of the examples provided. They are very common in people struggling with emotions. Start being the hero of your story by finding your reasons to stop avoiding and start living.

Reasons for Making Change Worksheet

Reason #1: _____

Reason #2: _____

Reason #3: _____

Reason #4: _____

Reason #5: _____

IDENTIFY YOUR STARTING POINT AND PREPARE FOR THE JOURNEY AHEAD

The final step is identifying your starting point. By recording where you are right now you can track how things change over time. Continuing the physical exercise example, it's similar to tracking how far you've gone after one run (0.5 miles in four minutes) to another run (1.0 mile in nine minutes) to yet another run (2.0 miles in twenty minutes). By tracking the distance and time, you can track your progress.

However, as discussed earlier, your anxiety and avoidance symptoms are much harder to measure. There is no simple blood test or distance measure to track your changes. Instead, the measurement of your symptoms will be focused on questionnaires. Some questionnaires run for pages and pages; I prefer to keep it short and sweet.

As you complete this questionnaire, you'll be setting the opening scene of your story. I will ask you to complete this same questionnaire in future chapters to track your progress as you continue on your journey through treatment. Once you've circled the numbers for the responses that correspond with your symptoms, please add up the response numbers to calculate your total score. And then turn to the Appendix 1 and enter your score and date in the Symptom Tracking Form. This form will help you to see how your symptoms change during the course of treatment. Additional copies of this form can be printed from http://www.newharbinger.com/45663.

Symptom Checklist	Not at all	A little	Moderately	Very much so
1. Depressed mood, most of the day, nearly every day	0	1	2	3
2. Avoidance of people, places, and situations (e.g., crowds)	0	1	2	3
3. Feeling constantly on guard and preparing for danger (e.g., back to the wall)	0	1	2	3
4. Frequent periods of intense anxiety or panic	0	1	2	3
5. Avoidance of physical sensations (e.g., heart racing, heavy breathing)	0	1	2	3
6. Avoidance of unpleasant thoughts or memories (e.g., of a car accident)	0	1	2	3
7. Loss of interest or pleasure, most of the day, nearly every day	0	1	2	3
8. Avoidance of activities that were previously enjoyed (e.g., working out)	0	1	2	3
Total Score:				
Date:				

WRAPPING UP

Okay, you've picked your goals for treatment, focused on your reasons for making these changes, and identified your starting point so you'll be able to know how far you've come when treatment is complete. Over the coming week, continue tracking your avoidance and also try to refer back to the goals you set in this chapter. Perhaps tear out your Reasons for Making Change Worksheet or make a copy and put it somewhere you can see often. See how it feels to refer to these goals after recording your behavior. By now you truly have started on your journey of challenging avoidance, withdrawal, and isolation to improve how you feel and the life you live.

In the next chapter you will begin working on challenging and eventually reversing your avoidance and isolation. You will be learning the tools that you need to get your life back. The technique that you'll learn is called *exposure*. It is one of the most powerful tools that we have in psychotherapy. And it is the solution that you've been searching for to stop avoiding and start living.

Learn How to Challenge Avoidance by Proving It Wrong

In the first two chapters, you focused on the connection between your avoidance and isolation and how you've been feeling. More specifically, we discussed your growing list of avoided activities and how they have been influencing your life, both the short-term positive effects as well as the long-term negative effects. We emphasized the importance of being on the lookout for avoidance and isolation throughout your day-to-day activities, preparing you to start going after it and tackling it head on. Keeping tabs on this will help you to know yourself well enough to anticipate avoidance, replace it, and ultimately defeat it.

Your next step was developing your goals for treatment. Just like any good hero in a story, you have to have a mission or goal to win the day. Rather than simply relying on wanting to "feel better" or "be less depressed," I challenged you to express your goals as observable changes. How would you look differently or behave differently as seen through a video camera if you felt less depressed, angry, or fearful? The goals that you set will be critical to knowing where to go with the exercise that you will be learning shortly.

Similar to setting your goals, you also identified your motivations for pushing through the challenges ahead to make your desired change. You outlined the *why* for reading this chapter, and the next, and the one after that (and for engaging in the activities contained in each). You should now know why you will continue reading this book to the end, challenge yourself to push through the exercises, and stop avoiding and start living.

Finally, you completed your first questionnaire rating of your symptoms; this creates a record of your starting point, which you can compare to later scores as we see how far you've gone or how you're changing as you move through the chapters and make progress along the way. You've set the opening scene of the story, identified your biggest obstacle (avoidance), and decided that you've had enough and you're ready to move forward to make a better life for yourself. Now, you are ready to start your journey through treatment.

This chapter will introduce you to the *how* in making this change for the better. It will be like the hero's sword in your story; it will be your primary tool to stop avoiding and start living. Namely, you will learn about exposures and how to use them to challenge your avoidance and isolation and reduce your negative emotions. Let's get started.

REVISITING THE AVOIDANCE TRAP

Before jumping into new material, let's briefly return to the initial model of avoidance and isolation that you learned in week 1, as it is very much related to what you'll learn in this chapter. In that model, an initial event or series of events leads you to experience negative emotions, such as fear, anxiety, or depression. Once you experience those initial negative emotions, you may begin to pull back from or avoid important people, tasks, and situations. We used the story of Mark as an example. You saw that the more that Mark pulled away, the worse he felt; and the worse he felt, the more he wanted to pull away. Over time, the negative emotions and avoidance and isolation had become so severe that Mark had lost his job and become estranged from his friends and family. Even though he was able to move on from his divorce after a couple of years, the cycle of negative emotions and avoidance and isolation continued to reinforce one another until he sought out treatment to learn how to stop avoiding and start living.

Now that we've discussed this model again, it's likely that you're starting to see patterns of avoidance and isolation in your day-to-day life. Since you have been filling in your Record of Avoided Situations Worksheet, you should be seeing avoidance around every corner by now.

This model may seem too simple. How, you may ask, could such a simple approach possibly be effective? Yes, it *is* simple, but for our purposes, that simplicity is its greatest strength. As you start this journey of change, the last thing you need is a complicated challenge.

That said, although the worksheet outlines what went wrong and what continues to plague you, it doesn't necessarily tell the entire story. Avoidance and isolation have more tricks to share. The next step or model dives a little deeper into understanding how avoidance and isolation work to become so strong in your life that they have essentially taken over.

DIVING DEEPER INTO THE AVOIDANCE/ISOLATION CYCLE

Now that you've recognized your avoidance and isolation, the next step in mounting a challenge to them is to understand them even better. I know, you've already read one chapter about negative emotions and avoidance and then a chapter about goal setting and motivation identification. Now, I'm starting this chapter by talking more about avoidance. I realize that this may feel like your first soccer or baseball practice as a child. The coach keeps going on and on about teamwork and having fun, while all of the kids just want to run and play with the balls. It's actually great that you are becoming eager to get on with it—to challenge your avoidance and isolation. In fact, maybe you've already started to do so on your own (and that's okay). I promise that we will reach the official starting point soon. And I also promise that it will be worth your while to learn a few more important points about avoidance and isolation.

This new model of avoidance and isolation focuses on the moment you decide to leave a situation or avoid it entirely. Figure 3.1 shows the model.

Figure 3.1. Avoidance/Isolation Model

Regular use of avoidance/isolation can result in a vicious cycle. Each time you rely on avoidance, you are making any future attempts to participate in activities more and more challenging over time, reinforcing your initial discomfort and making it more difficult to learn information to counter your avoidance and isolation.

1. As you approach a stressful situation, you tend to feel more negative emotions. And as soon as the situation actually begins, those negative emotions may increase further and faster.

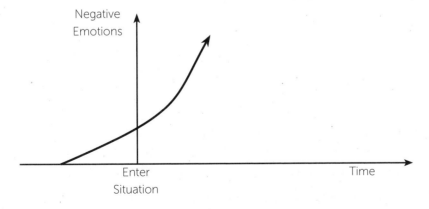

2. When you escape/avoid the situation, the initial negative emotions decrease rapidly and you experience the short-term benefits of avoidance/isolation.

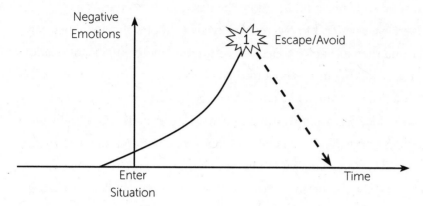

3. However, the more you escape/avoid, the more you will want to escape/avoid in the future. It becomes the easy way out. In addition, your negative emotions come faster and are harder to overcome. Over time, you come to rely on escape/avoid before the situation even begins.

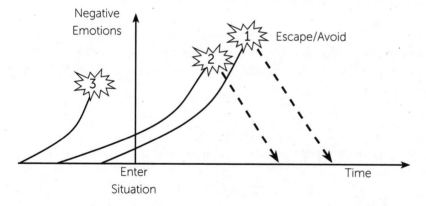

Now, whenever you enter a stressful situation, you begin to experience rapidly increasing negative emotions. The dark clouds seem to follow you everywhere. And as these negative emotions continue, your urge to avoid grows as well. Ultimately, these strong emotions may lead you to leave or escape the situation in order to get the short-term benefit of reduced negative emotions. However, the cycle does not stop there; it learns to get stronger. Namely, your initial use of avoidance to cope results in stronger negative emotions and a stronger urge to escape when you return to the stressful situation, leading you to leave the situation again (and sooner than the previous encounter). Eventually, these negative emotions and urges to escape become strong enough that you avoid the situation altogether and you experience the long-term negatives of avoidance. Avoidance has won the day.

Mark's Story (continued)

We have spoken about Mark a few times now. Let's apply his story to this new model of avoidance and isolation. Mark's difficulties at work offer a great example for this model. After Mark's wife left him, he began to experience strong negative emotions when completing activities that previously did not bother him, such as going to work or spending time with friends. Much of Mark's initial negative emotions centered on sadness and anger, as well as shame and embarrassment. As for going to work, Mark's negative emotions began as soon as he got up in the morning. He had to drag himself out of bed, shave and shower, get dressed, have breakfast, and then leave for the day. As he completed each task, his negative emotions and his urge to avoid grew. At first, Mark was able to struggle through the work day. That was until Mark decided to use avoidance. One day at work, Mark got a text from his wife, arguing about their pending divorce, and his sadness and anger were too much to handle. He had had enough. He grabbed his things and left work for the day. The act of leaving (avoidance) gave him immediate relief from the pressures of work and interacting with coworkers (short-term benefit). Sure, it didn't fix his problems with his soon-to-be ex-wife (and it left work tasks undone), but it felt good to get away from everything and just go home and drink a beer or four (more avoidance).

Over time, Mark began to leave work more and more frequently, from once weekly to several days a week. His departure time also crept to an earlier and earlier point in the day, starting with taking the last couple of hours off, later planning to work only a half day, and finally staying home altogether. Eventually, Mark skipped his morning routine of preparing for work and just stayed in bed, sometimes hungover from all of the drinking from the previous night (when he knew that he probably wouldn't be going to work anyway).

In the end, his avoidance had won. He quit his job, blaming his ex-wife's behaviors and his boss's insensitivity to his problems (longer-term negatives). But of course, quitting his job and staying home did not improve his negative emotions. His depression and anger continued to get worse with each step. Mark had removed his perceived negatives of going to work and completing his tasks, but he also removed the positive emotions associated with his many former accomplishments in his job as well as his friendly interactions with his coworkers. And the financial stressors that contributed to Mark's marital distress were not improved by losing his job. Bottom line, Mark's use of avoidant behaviors made his situation and related negative emotions much, much worse.

With this model and Mark's example, I hope you are understanding the role (and the negative influence) of avoidance and isolation in your life.

Can you think of more situations that you have begun to avoid over time?

_____

_____

Are there things that you used to do that you have simply given up on due to your negative emotions?

_____

_____

Whenever such things come to mind, be sure to add them to your Record of Avoided Situations Worksheet. As you will see, it will be very useful to have a list of situations to target and eventually overcome with exposures.

PROVING YOUR AVOIDANCE WRONG WITH EXPOSURES

Okay, it is finally the time to talk about exposures. Exposure is the most effective tool you can use to move ahead with breaking free of your avoidance/isolation trap. I've referred to exposure throughout the discussion of emotions. We have been homing in on the villains of your story: avoidance and isolation. By gaining this clearer picture of how they have become entrenched in your life, I hope that you now both (1) understand the connections between your use of avoidance and isolation and their impact on your negative emotions *and* (2) are quite ready to do something about it.

Let's start with a basic example of how exposures work. I like to introduce them in the simplest terms possible. Exposure is a fairly straightforward concept that makes a lot of sense, but simply describing how it works can generate negative emotions. And so, I will start with a type of negative emotion (fear) that most people can understand, and the source of the negative emotion (cats) being something that generally doesn't cause that negative emotion in most people.

Tommy's Story

Tommy is a nine-year-old boy who lives a few doors down from you. Tommy is a good kid that always says hi when riding by on his bike and offers help when he sees you need it, such as helping to carry your shopping bags inside. Tommy seems like a pretty normal kid, and he is, but one day he shares a problem with you. It turns out that Tommy really does not like cats. In fact, Tommy is scared of cats, to the point of having a real phobia. Sure, you've noticed once or twice how Tommy has gone out of his way to stay away from the home of another neighbor who lets her cat outside, or you've even seen him stop his bike and turn around when that cat is sitting near the sidewalk. But you never gave it much thought. Well today, Tommy makes you think about it.

Tommy asks whether you like cats. And have you've ever heard of cat scratch fever? He tells you how his aunt's cat scratched him once when he was little. Although this little scratch didn't need anything more than a bandage and a kiss from his mom, Tommy says that he won't go to his aunt's house anymore. She lives several states away, so it doesn't really come up.

Then Tommy says that his best friend, George, that kid you often see with Tommy, just got a cat, and Tommy doesn't know what to do. He feels like he can't go to George's house anymore. No more all-day video game battles in George's basement. No more pizza and movie nights with George's family. And definitely no more sleepovers at George's house. For Tommy, the new cat has ruined everything. He asks if *you'll* be his new best friend. Although you are honored by the request, you offer to help Tommy get over his fear so he can resume all of his fun with George.

Who is the villain in Tommy's story? Or more specifically, what strategy is Tommy using to cope with his negative emotions (and temporary lack of positive emotions)? Do you think that the short-term benefits of Tommy's behavior outweigh the long-term consequences of losing his best friend?

I hope that by now the answers to these questions are fairly easy for you. In fact, I didn't provide an area for you to write them, because I *know* that you know them by now. Tommy is, of course, using avoidance to try to cope (ineffectively) with his fear of cats. If he stays away, he does not feel the fear and discomfort associated with the cat (short-term benefit). But at the same time, Tommy has acknowledged the long-term negative effects associated with his strategy (losing his best friend and needing to find a new one).

Now let's turn to another set of questions, which I *do* want you to answer. What would you recommend that Tommy do to help reduce his fear of cats? What strategy could he use to feel better over time and resume his friendship with George?

_____

_____

_____

That's right: Tommy can face his fears by confronting his avoidance and getting used to the cat. More specifically, Tommy needs to spend increasing time with the cat to learn whether it is in fact dangerous or not (exposure). He needs to visit with the cat over and over until he learns whether his fears (of getting scratched or hurt) will come true. He needs to learn whether his fears are accurate. And, whether they are or not, he needs to learn how bad it actually could be if they are true. Put a different way, would a superficial cat scratch be so bad (requiring a bandage and another kiss from Mom) that it is worth the consequences of continued avoidance (losing a best friend)? Or are his fear and anxiety so bad that it is worth losing a best friend over rather than pushing through them?

Now we'll use this example to look at a new model, focused on exposure: Using Exposure to End the Avoidance/Isolation Cycle (figure 3.2). Let's see how this model compares to the model of avoidance and isolation.

USING EXPOSURE TO END THE AVOIDANCE/ISOLATION CYCLE

In contrast to the avoidance/isolation cycle, in which escape/avoidance reduces initial negative emotions (short-term) and encourages future avoidance (long-term), we can use exposure to challenge the feared negative outcomes (short-term) to reduce negative emotions and improve positive emotions (long-term). Exposure enables us to fight back and end the cycle of avoidance.

Figure 3.2. Using Exposure to End the Avoidance/Isolation Cycle

1. Negative emotions tend to increase as you anticipate negative outcomes.

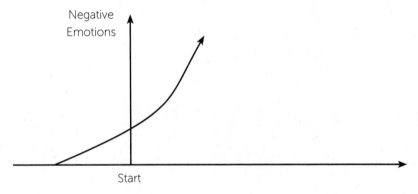

2a. If you instead stay put and face the situation, you challenge your anticipated negative outcome and learn from the experience. As a result, your negative emotions may level out and reduce over time.

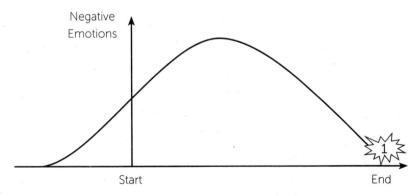

2b. Even if your negative emotions aren't reduced, you will learn from challenging your anticipated negative outcome and prepare yourself for future exposures.

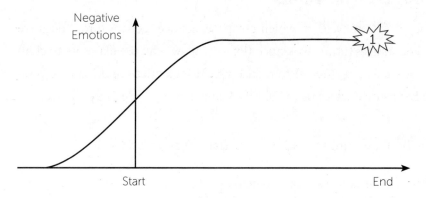

3. With either a peak (2a) or plateau (2b), you learn a new way to approach and manage these situations as you continue to challenge your anticipated negative outcome. Over time, your negative emotions will become less and less impairing.

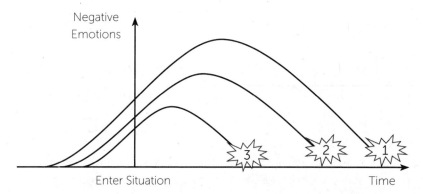

4. In addition to the likely effects of repeated exposures on negative emotions, the effects on your anticipated negative outcome also can lead to increased positive emotions over time.

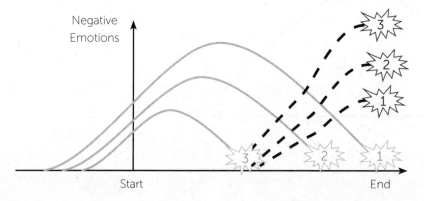

As with the avoidance/isolation model, immediate and intense negative emotions begin and increase rapidly when you enter into the situation (see #1). However, unlike with the avoidance model, you elect to *stay* in the situation and *expose* yourself to the related emotions. As you can see from the illustration (see #2a), your negative emotions will peak (highest point) and then slowly begin to pass (reduce) as you learn the outcome of staying. Alternatively (see #2b), your negative emotions may peak (highest point) and plateau (remain at highest point) and still allow you to learn the outcome of staying. As we discussed in week 1, you know that nothing bad can happen to us physically from strong negative emotions (no heart attack or stroke). With this perceived risk removed, you are free to get used to the situation and learn the outcome.

Let's return to our example of Tommy and his fear of cats. If Tommy volunteers to go into a room with George's cat, at first, he will be afraid and tense because he is around the cat (see #1). However, as Tommy remains in the room and nothing seriously bad happens, Tommy will eventually get used to the cat, and his negative emotions will reduce (see #2a).

After completing your own first exposure to a situation you have been avoiding, you will be left with new information:

1. You will learn that the situation really was not dangerous or even that unpleasant, and there was no physical danger from your negative emotions (heart attack or breakdown).

2. You will learn that you can *tolerate* highly negative emotions and that they may eventually peak and pass over time.

3. This information will leave you with a very different impression. Rather than thinking that you cannot handle the situation and that you have to use avoidance to feel better, you likely will leave thinking that it was hard, but it was doable—and it will get better over time.

Circle your choices:

If Tommy stayed in the room for a half hour or even an hour and began to feel more at ease with the cat, how would he feel about visiting the cat again?

more uncomfortable   less uncomfortable

Would he be more or less likely to go back to George's house?

less likely   more likely

Would he be more or less likely to start having fun with George again?

less likely   more likely

Clearly one key element of the exposure model is repeated practice. After staying long enough to learn the outcome of your first practice, your second practice should be a little easier to approach, with less severe negative emotions (see #3). Your third practice is even less difficult, and so on from there (see #3). Better still, you should experience both a reduction in negative emotions as well as an increase in positive emotions as you begin to enjoy the situations once more (having fun going out with friends or family, watching a sporting event, or completing a difficult task) (see #4).

So what happens to Tommy? It turns out that Tommy takes your advice, challenges his fear of cats, and learns that nothing bad happens. The cat doesn't bite or scratch (and even if it did, he knows that it won't be serious). And Tommy manages his fear well. When he goes back, Tommy thinks that the cat may be just as harmless, but he is still cautious. He lets his anxiety peak and pass and is ready for his next visit, until over time the cat doesn't bother Tommy any longer and, more importantly, Tommy and George are best buddies again and having fun no matter where they play. Tommy has successfully stopped avoiding and started playing again.

PLANNING YOUR FIRST EXPOSURE PRACTICE

Okay, let's get started with exposure.

Pick something on your avoided situations list to try an initial exposure. Your goal, this week, will be to simply *try* the activity and complete the Initial Exposure Practice Worksheet that follows. Additional copies can be printed from http://www.newharbinger.com/45663. You should focus on selecting an activity that you will be able to try, rather than picking the biggest, and baddest activity. Just like in an action movie, the hero starts with the henchmen before working their way up to the boss.

Once you have chosen your first exposure activity, give it a go as soon as you get the chance. You can either preset the day and time or fill these in after your attempt. Later in treatment, scheduling will be key to getting things done, but that can wait for another day, if necessary.

The worksheet asks you to track your emotions during the exposure, including how you are feeling at the beginning, peak, and end of the exercise. Try to notice and take mental note of any physical sensations, negative thoughts, or behaviors experienced during the exposure exercise so you can record them as soon as you're able. Also, take note of the total time you spend on the exposure practice. Taken all together, this information will be critical to planning new exposures on your journey to stop avoiding and start living.

Initial Exposure Practice

Planned Initial Exposure: _____

Date/Time	Initial Emotions −100 (neg) to +100 (pos)	Peak Emotions −100 (neg) to +100 (pos)	Final Emotions −100 (neg) to +100 (pos)	Total Time Engaged in Exposure
Physical Sensations What are you feeling?	Negative Thoughts What are you thinking?	Behaviors What are you doing?		

WRAPPING UP

We will be discussing exposure practices in more detail in the next chapter, but before you read it, it's important for you to get at least a general sense of the practice. You have a new tool; give it a try this week before moving on to week 4. While I hope that Tommy's example was helpful, it's going to be much more helpful to have your *own* experience to contemplate and connect to the future descriptions of exposure.

In the next chapter, we will continue to talk about exposure and how to apply it to your experience of emotions. It's one thing to find a sword, but you need to learn how to wield it. We will review your first exposure practice—that's why you need to try one before reading further. We also will get more into the details of exposure and how to perfect its use to challenge your avoidance. This will prepare you to shift your exposure practice into a higher gear.

Let's do this. I know that it will work for you.

Begin Your Exposure Practices

We have spent three chapters and as many weeks now talking about all of the problems associated with avoidance and isolation. You've learned the reasons why you started to use it, the short-term positives associated with avoidance that have reinforced your use, and the interplay between emotions and avoidance. At this point, I hope and expect that you are tired of both learning about avoidance and isolation, as well as the actual extent of avoidance and isolation in your day-to-day life. This is an exciting moment: you've had enough of avoidance. You are tired of seeing avoidance win in your story. At this point, I know that you are ready to take on the next challenge and begin to stop avoiding and start living again. So let's quickly check in with your symptoms.

RESETTING THE SCENE TO IDENTIFY TARGETS AND PREPARE FOR THE JOURNEY AHEAD

To help you track the effects of your planned exposures, you will be monitoring symptoms of negative emotions throughout this treatment. We need to reset to see where you are now, compared to where you've been on your journey—even a few weeks in, it is possible to see some changes. Remember our earlier physical exercise example. This form for tracking your negative emotions and use of avoidance works similarly to that tracking of your exercise distance and time.

Begin by completing and scoring the questionnaire, then enter your score and today's date in the Appendix 1 Symptom Tracking Form. This form will help you to see how your symptoms change during the course of treatment.

Symptom Checklist	Not at all	A little	Moderately	Very much so
1. Depressed mood, most of the day, nearly every day	0	1	2	3
2. Avoidance of people, places, and situations (e.g., crowds)	0	1	2	3
3. Feeling constantly on guard and preparing for danger (e.g., back to the wall)	0	1	2	3
4. Frequent periods of intense anxiety or panic	0	1	2	3
5. Avoidance of physical sensations (e.g., heart racing, heavy breathing)	0	1	2	3
6. Avoidance of unpleasant thoughts or memories (e.g., of a car accident)	0	1	2	3
7. Loss of interest or pleasure, most of the day, nearly every day	0	1	2	3
8. Avoidance of activities that were previously enjoyed (e.g., working out)	0	1	2	3
Total Score:				
Date:				

How'd you do? Did your score change since your recording in week 2? Circle your response.

No Change or Symptoms Worsening   Symptom Improvement

No Change or Symptoms Worsening: Please do not get discouraged if you fall into this category. Despite taking in lots of new information and monitoring your symptoms, you haven't been asked to do much in terms of strategies to challenge your avoidance (and therefore starting to achieve your treatment goals). If anything, all of the learning and monitoring your symptoms may have improved your awareness of your avoidance (which is a good thing for making change) and caused you to rate your avoidance and related symptoms as worse now than you would have previously. Please be patient, and rest assured that changes will come soon.

Symptom Improvement: Honestly, it surprises me when patients start to show improvements at this very early phase in the treatment process. It is not impossible or even that uncommon. But, it tends to be associated with aspects the patient's life that we haven't yet directly addressed in treatment. You may have gained improved understanding of avoidance and isolation and how to challenge them, and this has raised your confidence and positive outlook toward the better future to come. Maybe the possibility of reaching a happy ending to your story has become more real for you. If that's the case, I'm very excited. That's a great place to be in. Confidence about making successful change will help you through your future exposure practices.

The other possible explanation is that you've already started to challenge avoidance on your own without waiting for me to direct you there. If so, I'm equally excited for you. Again, the goal of the first couple of chapters was to label avoidance and isolation as the villains, making them so unpleasant that you couldn't wait to start to fight back. If that sounds like you, I encourage you to keep reading.

Whatever the change (or lack of change) and whatever the reasons for said change (or lack of it), I'm very happy that you are continuing to read on and work through this treatment program. We will revisit this questionnaire again and again, as we check your progress on your journey. As long as you keep working the program, you should start to see the improvements.

YOUR FIRST EXPOSURE

We began to talk about exposure in the last chapter. Exposure is the driving force for change in this treatment approach. As the hero of your story, exposure will be your best tool in overcoming the avoidance and isolation that have taken control of your life. The chapter ended with instructions and an Initial Exposure Practice Worksheet. If you haven't yet tried your first exposure practice, it's essential that you do so before continuing with this chapter.

What exposure did you try?

_____

_____

Great job trying your first exposure! That is a significant accomplishment, no matter the outcome. Again, the goal of the exercise was for you to try to challenge your avoidance by confronting a situation that you typically avoid. That is not an easy thing to try, as you likely learned. You tried to challenge your long-standing pattern of avoidance and isolation. That really is a big deal.

You may have noticed that I kept repeating one word over and over in this paragraph: *try*. I did that to emphasize a point: you *tried* to challenge your avoidance. I'm not complimenting your mastery of exposures, or your crossing off of an item on your Record of Avoided Situations Worksheet. Rather, at this point it is all about your *making the effort*.

Let's take this opportunity to quickly look back at the illustration for Using Exposure to End the Avoidance/Isolation Cycle in the previous chapter. In that model, improvements did not occur after a single exposure. It is only through repeated tries that you experience reductions in your avoidance and related negative emotions (see #3). And while the (overly simple) model shows it happening rapidly after three exposures (spoiler alert), it is likely going to take days or even weeks of exposure practices to (1) fight through the urge to avoid, (2) reduce your experience of negative emotions, and (3) fully experience positive emotions in these situations. During those practices, there will be some tough exposures and some easy exposures. There will be exposures that work well, and others that still result in lapses into avoidance. We will get to all that in the coming chapters. But for now, let's celebrate your first *try* at exposure. It is another critical step in your journey to stop avoiding and start living.

As for the attempt itself, here are some questions to consider about your exposure:

What made it challenging?

_____

_____

Did it activate your negative emotions?   Yes   No

What negative emotions did it activate?

_____

_____

What did you think in advance would happen? Did it happen the way that you thought it would?

_____

_____

What physical sensations, thoughts, and behaviors were pushing you to avoid?

_____

_____

Was there anything you found helpful in convincing you to stay?

_____

_____

Why did the exposure end?

_____

_____

How did you feel at the end of the experience?

_____

I hope that your first *try* at exposure was an eye-opening experience in terms of taking steps to challenge your negative emotions and start to work toward the goals that you identified in week 2.

LEARNING HOW TO GET EXPOSURE TO WORK FOR YOU

Let's go deeper into the exposure experience. Exposures have been shown to work in lots of different situations for many different types of challenges. They can vary in duration, time, location, and frequency. For example, some practices can be completed on your own at home, while others require interactions with other people or places. Some practices are very lengthy (hours at a time), while others are short (a few minutes at a time). Other differences exist in: how frequent the exposures are practiced (3 times a week versus twice a day), how exposures are selected (working up from the easiest to hardest activities versus bouncing between easy, moderate, and hard activities), how many types of exposures are practiced (one activity repeated until better versus many diverse activities practiced throughout), and how the exposure is practiced (by yourself versus with a friend or family member). As you can see, there is a lot of variability.

Exposure Rules

As many and varied as the possibilities are, we have learned through much experience that there are certain ways to make your exposure success more likely. We will call these techniques the *exposure rules*.

RULE #1: PRACTICES SHOULD BE PLANNED, STRUCTURED, AND PREDICTABLE.

You need to decide in advance when you will do the exposure, what you will do, and how long you will try it. We will discuss this more when planning your next exposures and using the Exposure Tracking Worksheet (which you'll find at the end of this chapter). The idea is that you should know what you're getting into, and you should have control of the situation.

You are the boss when it comes to planning these activities, and it needs to remain that way. I have had a number of patients in the past with an overly eager spouse or best friend who pushed them into exposures for which they were not prepared (one patient's boyfriend locked her in a small closet to force her to overcome her fear of enclosed spaces). These exposures tend to end up going very poorly and with less desired outcomes (I'm sorry to say that same patient broke up with the boyfriend, justifiably and understandably, and she experienced increased avoidance for the following weeks, to the point of even avoiding our appointments). It is wonderful to have support during this process, but it should remain just that—*support*—and never a forceful push.

RULE #2: HAVE A BACKUP PLAN.

Another good idea is to have a backup plan in case the original plan for an exposure practice does not work out (it rains, the store is closed, your friend isn't available). Sometimes the best-laid plans are thwarted by circumstances outside of our control, such as the weather. But, your success should not be dependent on the weather or a friend's availability. You have waited long enough to challenge your avoidance; you shouldn't have to wait on others to get better. You are taking action to get your life back. Setting a Plan B will help to ensure that you will be trying your exposure, rain or shine.

RULE #3: EXPECT TO FEEL UNCOMFORTABLE IN THE SITUATION.

Since you usually avoid these things, you *will* feel uncomfortable when you expose yourself to them. Whether the emotional response that your practices trigger is mild, moderate, or strong, you know that the exposure is working if you experience negative emotions. Of course this means that if you *don't* experience any negative emotions, you may need to revisit your selected exposures and move on to other avoided situations.

This idea of feeling discomfort is just like working out at the gym. You need to feel some strain to have a successful workout. The strain may be caused by lifting a heavier weight, increasing the length of your run, or increasing the frequency or speed of your workout. You may feel out of breath, get your heart rate up to a new high, or feel fatigue in some muscles. The point is that you have to push yourself to improve. For example, you wouldn't work out with five-pound weights if you are strong enough to lift a fifty-pound bag of dog food. You shouldn't pick easy exposures (things that you normally do already) and expect to see improvements. You need to find a good starting point that will challenge you and work your way up from there.

However, there is one important way in which exposures differ from working out. When working out, you can overdo it and hurt yourself by trying to lift too much or run too hard. Fortunately, exposures rarely carry the same risk. As we discussed in week 1, most negative emotions are not dangerous, even in the most severe presentations such as panic attacks. The one exception is suicidal feelings. Although very unlikely to be associated with exposure practices, again, if any such feelings arise you must take them very seriously and immediately seek care (see the contact information in week 1 under "Episodes involving suicidal and homicidal thoughts").

RULE #4: KEEP TRACK OF YOUR EMOTIONS BEFORE, DURING, AND AFTER EXPOSURE PRACTICES.

As we discussed when assigning your first exposure, you should keep track of your emotions throughout the practice. This can be completed in your head or on your Exposure Tracking Worksheet. You did this in your first exposure effort, and you will continue it with each of your future exposure practices. You simply need to ask yourself about your level of emotions every five minutes or so. At a minimum, try to identify your emotions at the start, at the peak or plateau, and at the end of the exposure. And be mindful to differentiate between negative and positive emotions. Increases in positive emotions during exposures will be discussed more in future chapters. This tracking will be important to know when you are ready to be done with your exposure (without using avoidance), which is described below.

RULE #5: DON'T USE SAFETY BEHAVIORS DURING YOUR EXPOSURES.

Before people enter treatment, they may have tried all kinds of things to work their way through avoided situations. One common example is consuming alcohol. Have you ever consumed a few beers before going out to "loosen up" or to make it easier to face the crowds or make the family event more enjoyable? There are many examples of safety behaviors, including recreational drugs (such as marijuana) and even some medications prescribed by doctors (commonly benzodiazepines, such as Xanax or Valium). Other examples of safety behaviors include ways that you approach an avoided situation, such as going to social gatherings only with your spouse, always keeping your back to the wall or keeping yourself in a position where you can observe the exits, or only going into public situations during off hours (going out to dinner at 4:30 p.m. or to a mid-day movie).

In many cases, these safety behaviors can jeopardize your learning during the exposure practices. Did you successfully stay in the crowded sporting event because you learned that it wasn't as bad as you expected (and your emotions improved), or was it because you drank three beers? That's a tough question to answer, and you can see how that coping strategy will blur your potential learning.

When it comes to drugs, alcohol, and select prescription medications (benzodiazepines), it is best for you to *not* to use them immediately before, during, or immediately after an exposure practice. It's important to consult your prescribing provider before discontinuing or adjusting the dosing of any prescribed medications.

There are a host of more subtle strategies that you may use, such as having your spouse or close friend accompany you on exposures, as a way of easing into more challenging exposures over time. Your treatment goal is not only to be able to do those activities with a friend close at hand; rather, you want to be able to do those things with or without company. If you need to, you can start your exposures with an "exposure buddy"—just as long as you adjust, over time, to doing them on your own. For example, on the first exposure, you can start by going to a store and shopping together with your buddy. For your next exposure, you return to the store, and you and your buddy shop separately in different parts of the store. After that, you return to the store and shop while your buddy shops in a neighboring store. And finally, you return to the store alone and complete your shopping. If you follow a sequence like this, you will learn that you can do it with or without help.

What safety behaviors have you used in the past? What behaviors should you try not to use during exposures?

_____

_____

RULE #6: EXPOSURE PRACTICE SHOULD LAST UNTIL YOU MEET YOUR KEY OBJECTIVES.

You need to stay in an exposure situation long enough to (1) learn the outcome of the exposure, (2) experience a significant decrease in your negative emotions, and (3) potentially experience positive emotions. This approach of sticking with it until your emotions peak and pass is depicted in figure 3.2, Using Exposure to End the Avoidance/Isolation Cycle. Rather than engaging in avoidance (and thereby exacerbating the urge to avoid future situations), you will be pushing yourself to stay in the situation, learn about the outcome of the exposure, and go into future exposures with improved confidence that they will result in a similar (positive) outcome. While the goal is less about the actual symptom reduction and more about the learning that nothing bad happened, you'll typically experience symptom reduction after the new learning sinks in.

This process may be one of the harder parts of exposure practices. Avoidance and isolation didn't take over and bring about all of your negative emotions in one day; it happened over time. It likely took repeated use of avoidance to get you to the point that you're at today, to the point at which you found this book. Now it's your job to go into these situations and stick with it until you are able to test your anticipated negative outcome. This may take ten minutes, thirty minutes, or longer. How are you going to accomplish this? For one, it will be helpful to remind yourself why you are doing all this. Think back to your reasons for making these changes outlined in week 2. Another helpful strategy is to take it one step, or minute, at a time. When you think you can't make it, try to stay in the situation just one minute more. Then for one minute more. Take it one minute at a time. You'll be surprised how many one minute mores you might be able to make it through. If ultimately you need to leave the situation before your negative beliefs are proven wrong, record your total time on your Exposure Tracking Worksheet and try to beat that time on your next exposure. Eventually, if you keep pushing your practices longer and longer, you will disprove your negative beliefs, feel less-severe negative emotions, and (potentially) begin to experience positive emotions.

Why are you doing this again? Why are you going to push through your avoidance?

_____

_____

RULE #7: EXPOSURE PRACTICES SHOULD BE REPEATED FREQUENTLY AND SPACED CLOSE TOGETHER.

The more frequently practiced and more closely spaced together that your exposures are, the greater the likelihood of influencing your negative beliefs, reducing your negative emotions, and increasing your positive emotions. It is a good practice to repeat the same exposure until your experience becomes easier. As with learning anything new, the more you practice, the better you'll get. If you want to learn to ice skate or play guitar or ride a bike, you should practice the skill frequently to see the most improvement. Would you expect to get better at ice skating by doing it only once a month, or at playing the guitar only when your friend comes over with his guitar (that is, only every so often, by chance)? The answer is *no*. You should schedule at least one or two exposures per day on your Exposure Tracking Worksheet. These exposures do not need to be the same exact situation, over and over (like going to the same store daily); rather, they should be the same *type* of situation, repeated frequently (walking through different stores daily). The more exposures that you complete, the faster you are going stop avoiding and start living.

PUTTING YOUR TRAINING TO GOOD USE

Now, it is time to put it all together. The Exposure Tracking Worksheet will be your weekly planner. Use it to schedule each of your exposures in advance and to track your progress along the way. Additional copies of this form can be printed from http://www.newharbinger.com/45663. You may find this task of planning a week's worth of activities intimidating at first. For some guidance and support, let's return to Mark's story to see how he met this challenge.

Mark's Story (continued)

Mark, you'll recall, was at one time a successful guy with a (seemingly) happy marriage and a fulfilling job. However, mounting financial pressures and frequent arguments with his wife resulted in the significant negative life events of separation and divorce. Mark began to feel depressed and angry and avoided his work responsibilities, friends, social activities, and family with increasing frequency, which in turn made his negative emotions worse. When he first arrived for treatment, Mark had moved on from this previous job and was working in a less-demanding (and lower-paying) job and spent most of his time isolated and depressed (and typically drunk).

Once Mark had (1) learned about the relation between his negative emotions and his avoidance and isolation, (2) understood his reasons for making change, (3) set his treatment goals, and (4) gained a good understanding of how he would use exposure to stop avoiding and start living, he was ready to plan out his weekly exposure exercises. Mark referenced his treatment goals (improving his work situation, reconnecting with family, and spending time out with friends and with hobbies) and his Record of Avoided Situations Worksheet (applying for new jobs, calling family and friends, going out with friends, crowded situations). And so, Mark began to list the exposure activities he planned to do later that week.

Mark's Exposure Tracking Worksheet

	Planned Exposure	Scheduled Day/Time	Initial Symptoms (–100 to +100)	Peak Symptoms (–100 to +100)	Final Symptoms (–100 to +100)	Total Time
1	Church	Sunday @ 10 a.m.				
2	Call Mom	Sunday @ 2 p.m.				
3	Fishing without beer	Sunday @ 4 p.m.				
4	Gym	Monday @ 7 a.m.				
5	Text friends for meetup	Monday @ 12 p.m.				
6	Grocery shopping	Monday @ 5 p.m.				
7	Morning run	Tuesday @ 7 a.m.				
8	Cook dinner without beer	Tuesday @ 6 p.m.				

9	Gym	Wednesday @ 7 a.m.						
10	Lunch with coworker	Wednesday @ 12 p.m.						
11	Call Dad without beer	Wednesday @ 8 p.m.						
12	Morning run	Thursday @ 7 a.m.						
13	Outing with friends with three–beer limit	Thursday @ 6 p.m.						
14	Gym	Friday @ 7 a.m.						
15	Bowling league with two–beer limit	Friday @ 6 p.m.						
16	Morning run	Saturday @ 7 a.m.						
17	Submit five job applications	Saturday @ 11 a.m.						
18	Beach walk without beer	Saturday @ 7 p.m.						

As you see, Mark planned a lot of activities. In fact, the goal of this treatment is to plan two or three exposures per day. Some will be brief activities (texting friends; calling a parent). Others will be more time consuming (fishing; bowling league night; completing job applications). And, although Mark planned eighteen exposures, the expectation was not 100-percent success. Prior to his exposures, Mark was doing very little, apart from working and watching television at home and drinking beer. *Any activities* that Mark completed would be an improvement over his current situation. And if he plans eighteen, he is more likely to complete more activities than if he plans only a couple of activities. Said differently, completing 50 percent of eighteen planned activities is going to be far more effective than completing 50 percent of three planned activities.

OVERCOMING COMMON FORMS OF RESISTANCE

It is likely at this stage of planning that your negative emotions are urging you start slowly or select only activities that you know that you'll do. That's a common hesitation—or better yet, trick to enable yourself to continue avoiding. While fewer commitments can spell fewer possible "failures," they also guarantee fewer successes. You're probably familiar with what hockey legend Wayne Gretzky observed: "You miss 100 percent of the shots that you don't take." If you don't try exposures, you won't improve your negative emotions. And I'll say it again: there are no failures at this point, as long as you keep *trying*.

The other frequent obstacle is the scheduling component. Again, your negative emotions are likely arguing for you to simply select a few exposures and not plan them, but do them whenever you get around to it (if you ever get around to it). That way, you can continue to put them off day after day until you realize that it's been a couple of weeks and you haven't tried any of them yet. I expect that's what you've been doing for a while now. Has that been working for you?

When thinking about scheduling activities, I like to use the following example. Let's say that you are sitting down at a blackjack table in a Las Vegas casino. For those of you unfamiliar with blackjack, the game involves getting two or more cards dealt to each player by the dealer. The dealer gives themselves two cards as well. The person with the score closest to 21 without going over wins whatever bets were placed on the game. Seems pretty simple, right? Well, it becomes even simpler in this example. The dealer sits down and makes you a special offer of choosing between two decks of cards.

- In deck 1, the dealer has shuffled the cards repeatedly and all players get random cards to start the game. This is the standard deck, and it's fairly standard for the casino to win in the end.

- In deck 2, the dealer will allow you to put the cards in any order that you like, without shuffling the cards afterward. The cards remain in whatever order you choose.

Which deck will you choose, and why?

_____

_____

Well, if it were me, I'd select that second deck. Putting the cards in the preferred order (scheduling exposures) greatly increases your chances of winning (engaging in planned exposures). Whereas with deck 1, you are allowing the cards to land as they may (no scheduling of exposures), and you are most likely to be broke in the end (avoidance keeps winning).

Mark's Story (continued)

Getting back to Mark: he ended up completing about half of his scheduled exposures. The morning workouts ended up being challenging (he did only two of seven) and he ended up drinking too much during the evening out with his old friends. But at the same time, Mark made great strides in reconnecting with family and friends and restarting a couple of long-lost hobbies. He applied for a better job, and most importantly, in the process of practicing scheduled exposures, he felt less negative and more positive. He acknowledged that he definitely would have put off calling his parents if they weren't on his list at specific times, and there was no way that he would have worked out at all if he hadn't specifically set his alarm for an earlier wake-up. In addition, Mark wouldn't have seen his friends on that Thursday night if he hadn't planned to text them on Monday afternoon to set up the outing. The point is: the more exposures you plan, the more likely it is that you will complete them and feel better.

SCHEDULING EXPOSURES

Now it's your turn. Per the Exposure Rules (and Mark's example), you need to select a diverse set of exposures to plan for the week. They should be both challenging and frequent. And you should plan them on specific days and times, with possible backup plans just in case something interferes. If you have any problematic safety behaviors, similar to Mark's beer drinking, please make note of how you'll manage them in at-risk exposures (for example, set a two-beer maximum and stick to it—unlike Mark). Your completed Record of Avoided Situations Worksheet and treatment goals (week 2) can be excellent resources for selecting exposures and prioritizing areas of improvement. Additional copies of the Exposure Tracking Worksheet can be printed from http://www.newharbinger.com/45663.

Exposure Tracking Worksheet

	Planned Exposure	Scheduled Day/Time	Initial Symptoms (−100 to +100)	Peak Symptoms (−100 to +100)	Final Symptoms (−100 to +100)	Total Time
Example	Shop at grocery store	Tuesday @ 2 p.m.	−50	−80	−40	45min
1						
2						
3						
4						
5						
6						
7						
8						

Planned Exposure	Scheduled Day/Time	Initial Symptoms (–100 to +100)	Peak Symptoms (–100 to +100)	Final Symptoms (–100 to +100)	Total Time
9					
10					
11					
12					
13					
14					
15					
16					
17					
18					

Now that your exposures are planned, it's time to start doing them. You may find it helpful to make a copy of your Exposure Tracking Worksheet and put it in a place that is hard to miss. In fact, I recommend that you make lots of copies and put them on your refrigerator, television, and bathroom mirror, by your alarm clock, and on your car dashboard. Another great option is to program each of the exposures on your smartphone calendar with obnoxious alarms and reminders. You should not forget about these, no matter what tricks your negative emotions may use to try to convince you otherwise. Remember, you are going to be the hero of this story. You now have your mission and your motivation, and the best tool for the job by your side. It is finally time for you to make real headway in transforming your life. This week may prove to be a very important turning point for you.

WRAPPING UP

In this chapter, you reviewed the model of avoidance and learned how to stop avoidance and isolation with the exposure model. You also reviewed your initial exposure practice and learned how to best use exposures to challenge your negative emotions. As you move day by day through the week, remember the rules: mainly, choose exposures that challenge you and practice them frequently, and stay long enough in each exposure to learn what really happens when you stay—typically, you will experience a reduction of negative emotions. Notice whether this happens for you or something else happens. By picking your first set of exposure practices for the coming week(s) and planning them on specific days and times, you have made a commitment to start fighting back against your avoidance and isolation and related negative emotions.

In the next chapter, we will continue our discussion of exposures, focusing on your exposure practices that you *tried* from this chapter. We will categorize your exposure successes and continued challenges, aiming to reinforce what worked and refine what still needs continued work. And you'll schedule another set of exposure practices to get you closer to your goal: to stop avoiding and start living.

Reinforce and Problem Solve Your Exposure Practices

You have completed five chapters, and you have reached the point at which treatment really gets moving. You have learned the basics of how exposures are used to end the cycle of avoidance and isolation and improve your related emotions. You have gone from tracking your avoidance to setting your treatment goals to trying your first exposure to now trying your first set of exposures. Although we still have several chapters remaining with valuable information for your journey to stop avoiding and start living, this chapter focuses on refining your exposure practice rather than introducing new skills or alternative approaches. The exposures can be extremely effective in improving your symptoms—but only if you are committed to them. It is not enough to just try one occasionally. You've likely been doing that on and off for years. The key is ongoing and repetitive practice.

This chapter is the first in a set of chapters in which you will work at refining your exposure practices. Because, as I've stressed, habit and repetition are key, these chapters follow a similar pattern:

1. Assess your symptoms and progress on your treatment goals.

2. Review your exposure practices by reinforcing and expanding your successes and problem solving your challenges.

3. Use the review to refine your exposure practices.

4. Assign your weekly exposure practices, incorporating the new refinements.

This pattern is intentional. It is meant to become your new routine. Recall the exercising example: you are most successful when working out becomes part of your normal routine. At first, it requires a big push just to get yourself to the gym and stay longer and longer until you are able to complete your full workout. Over time, it gets easier to get to the gym and finish your workout. If you keep with the program and don't experience any unexpected setbacks (illness or injury), working out becomes part of your normal weekly routine, no different than waking up, showering, and getting ready for work. And in fact, it begins to infiltrate other areas of your life without your realizing it, such as picking more active hobbies (going for a hike on vacation) or selecting healthier dinner options (choosing the grilled chicken sandwich over the double bacon cheese burger).

This pattern can be applied to exposures as well. Honestly, that has been my plan for you all along. Right now, you are likely forcing yourself to hang in there and complete exposures. Every practice is a challenge to start, with your avoidance screaming at you to simply do it later (until later becomes never). Avoidance is full of tricks. However, if you keep pushing, exposures will get easier to start and easier to complete. And if you keep at it, exposures will become your new routine. You will become less avoidant and isolated and more active without even realizing it. You will simply select activities because they are associated with positive emotions, as you've moved past the negative emotions that have stood in your way. This is the treatment plan. You are on your way. You've got this. Let's keep it going.

What are you looking forward to doing again as you begin to overcome your avoidance? Consistent with your treatment goals and motivations for treatment, what activities will get you closer to the life that you want for yourself again?

_____

_____

_____

As you reflect on what activities you are looking forward to doing again, make a note to include them when you pick your next exposures at the end of this chapter. Your exposures should be both practical and self-esteem building (such as shopping at the grocery store) and enjoyable and mood improving (such as catching up with old friends). Don't let avoidance stop you.

RESETTING THE SCENE TO IDENTIFY TARGETS AND PREPARE FOR THE JOURNEY AHEAD

Please complete and score the questionnaire and enter your score and today's date in the Appendix 1 Symptom Tracking Form. This will be your third score. Over time, you will be filling up that form in the Appendix and hopefully noticing significant changes in your symptoms and your progress on your treatment goals to stop avoiding and start living again.

Symptom Checklist	Not at all	A little	Moderately	Very much so
1. Depressed mood, most of the day, nearly every day	0	1	2	3
2. Avoidance of people, places, and situations (e.g., crowds)	0	1	2	3
3. Feeling constantly on guard and preparing for danger (e.g., back to the wall)	0	1	2	3
4. Frequent periods of intense anxiety or panic	0	1	2	3
5. Avoidance of physical sensations (e.g., heart racing, heavy breathing)	0	1	2	3
6. Avoidance of unpleasant thoughts or memories (e.g., of a car accident)	0	1	2	3
7. Loss of interest or pleasure, most of the day, nearly every day	0	1	2	3
8. Avoidance of activities that were previously enjoyed (e.g., working out)	0	1	2	3
Total Score:				
Date:				

How'd you do? Did your score change from the other scores? There are several possible outcomes here that we should discuss.

Symptom Worsening or No Change   Symptom Improvement

Symptom Worsening or No Change: Please do not get discouraged if you fall into this category. You have only just started with your exposure practices. At this point in treatment, we don't necessarily expect symptom improvements. We can return to the workout comparison. When you first start going to the gym, do you expect drastic changes to your physical health and fitness to happen immediately? Would you, for instance, expect to finish a fast mile after your first run in years? Of course not. If anything, those first workouts are generally associated with feeling worse than you did before you started. You'll likely feel sore and tight, maybe in a good bit of pain, but knowing that the aches and pains are a sign that your workouts will help you feel better in the future. Exposures work in a similar fashion. At the beginning (which you are at right now), your exposure practices may be associated with increased negative emotions (frustration, irritability, sadness, anxiety) and a big complaint from your avoidance. Just as I explained in the Exposure Rules in week 4, you will feel uncomfortable during your exposures (if you're doing them correctly). And, as you do more and more exposures, initially you will feel more negative emotions. Although this can be discouraging, it's how the process works. I urge you to be patient. Your hard work will pay off, and changes will come. Just keep at it.

Symptom Improvement: Even though you're picking up steam, symptom improvements are not necessarily expected at this phase in treatment (but if they happen, they are of course very welcome). However, keep in mind that you have attempted your first set of exposure practices, and early successes could lead to your feeling better (reduced negative emotions from successful practices, improved confidence and hopefulness for future successes, increased positive emotions experienced during the exposures themselves). If that's the case for you, that is very exciting news. I cannot promise that all practices will work the same way, nor can I promise that there won't be setbacks during the process, but early improvements are a promising sign of changes to come. Please keep reading and working toward your goals by scheduling and completing your exposures. You should continue to see improvements and get closer to your treatment goals as we go.

Whatever the change (or lack of change) and whatever the reasons for said change (or lack of it), I remain impressed by your persistence and fight to work through this treatment program. I hope you feel proud of your effort as well. As is the case for learning anything new, you will get as much out of it that you put in. As long as you keep working the program, you should see improvements related to getting closer and closer to your treatment goals to stop avoiding and start living.

REVIEWING LAST WEEK'S EXPOSURE PRACTICES

In the previous chapter, you assigned yourself a set of exposure practices on specific days and times. Following the exposure guidelines, you selected activities that you expected to cause you to experience negative emotions, and you did your best to stay in the exposures long enough to learn from the experience and potentially notice a reduction in your negative emotions (and an increase in your positive emotions) along the way. You also selected similar activities or the same activities more than once, giving yourself a chance to apply the learning from one exposure to the next exposure. And you did all of these things while trying not to use potential safety behaviors, such as needing to bring along a friend or family member or needing to drink alcohol to complete the exposure.

So how did it go?

Describe your overall experience, writing down the most important elements.

_____

_____

_____

Thinking back to your hopes and expectations, did it go exactly as you planned?

_____

_____

_____

To be honest, I wouldn't expect it to go like you thought it would. Remember, you are attempting to change a long-standing pattern of avoidance and isolation. This pattern did not appear overnight; it developed over time in response to negative life events, stressors, or trauma, with negative emotions and avoidance and isolation feeding each other to reach impairing levels over the course of months, years, or even decades. And with each experience of negative emotions, your continued use of avoidance and isolation rewarded you with the short-term benefit of reduced negative emotions (and a lot of long-term problems). Changing this pattern is not going to be easy or immediate, and your efforts to do so will be challenging. But, you have just taken another big step toward your goals to stop avoiding and start living again.

Let's take a closer look at your exposure practices. There are a few common outcomes for people when they start exposure work. I have detailed the most likely outcomes here. I expect that your experiences will fall into one or more of these categories. Review your exposure tracking form and match up your practices to these categories. Investigating your techniques and experiences should help you to better understand what happened in each of your attempts, problem solve any challenges, and prepare you to select your next set of practices in the exposure tracking form at the end of this chapter. It is rare to overcome avoidance after only one week. But with practice and problem solving, you will start to win, day after day and week after week, until you reach your treatment goals and your struggle with avoidance is over for years to come.

Possible Outcome #1: You tried some exposures and did not experience negative emotions.

Write down the exposures that you sailed through.

_____

_____

_____

Yes, even at this early stage, it is possible to try some exposures and not notice any increases in negative emotions (or positive emotions). This means that you may not have set the bar high enough in these practices. This would be similar to going to the gym and lifting only five pounds or doing only a few repetitions, when you are strong enough to do much more. This is going to happen sometimes with exposures; in fact, this should happen with increasing frequency as you continue to practice and feel better (get stronger) along the way. But for now, it is too early in treatment for you to be "all better" (unfortunately). You need to push yourself harder and pick more challenging exposures.

There is another possible explanation for the lack of negative emotions: the use of safety behaviors. We discussed safety behaviors, such as being accompanied by a family member or friend or being under the influence of alcohol, in the previous chapter. These are strategies that you may have used to handle these challenging situations in the past, as they kept your negative emotions in check. However, at the same time, they reinforced your avoidance and isolation (*I can go out and see my family only if I finish three beers first*). Think back and investigate the exposure that you tried that did not cause negative emotions; can you identify any safety behaviors that you relied on to get through the practice?

My safety behaviors included... _____

_____

_____

If you found any safety behaviors, try to remove them from your future practices. For example, if you did your shopping exposures only with your spouse (and felt fine doing so), schedule shopping exposures alone on your next exposure tracking form.

Possible Outcome #2: You tried some exposures and learned a little from them (almost stayed long enough).

For which exposures did you push yourself and stay, but ultimately walk away feeling that it didn't make a big difference in the end?

_____

_____

_____

This is a good starting point. You completed an exposure and experienced initial negative emotions (peak), but you did not experience any significant new learning regarding the expected negative outcome and never quite felt better (no pass). You tried to stand up to your avoidance, and you did, but you're not convinced that it will work every time. This is a common reaction early in exposure practices. It is okay for this to happen. In fact, it is good for it to happen now. The most important part is that you *tried* the exposure practice and that you were able to *stay in the situation.* If you continue to challenge your negative beliefs, I promise that your experience will change and your negative emotions will reduce, along with your urges to avoid and isolate.

Thinking about this exposure experience: what do you think happened this time to get in the way of greater change?

_____

_____

_____

_____

There are several possible explanations. First, your negative emotions may not reduce if your sense of your anticipated negative outcome is vague or unknown altogether. Although we haven't spent much time focused on identifying the anticipated negative outcome in the previous chapters, this is important, as uncertainty about this can keep you from challenging your avoidance and isolation (protecting your negative emotions), and being clear about the negative outcomes you anticipate is the key to overcoming them (improving your negative emotions). These anticipated negative outcomes tend to be very specific to each person, so knowing yours is important. Think back to the example in week 3, in which Tommy was afraid that a cat would hurt him if he stayed long enough. Once he stayed in the situation (instead of avoiding or escaping), Tommy learned that the cat was completely uninterested in him and did not in fact hurt him. That knowledge made it easier for Tommy to repeat the exposure until he no longer feared the cat.

Circle your responses to these questions about the negative outcomes that you anticipate might happen if you stayed long enough in your own exposures to experience a positive change.

Are you afraid that you will embarrass yourself?

Yes   No

Are you nervous that you will get angered and confront or fight someone?

Yes   No

Are you afraid that you will be attacked or that there will be a random act of violence such as a mass shooting?

      Yes   No

Are you afraid that you will become overwhelmed and lose control?

      Yes   No

Are you fearful of becoming so anxious that you have a panic attack and die from an associated heart attack or stroke? (Reminder: panic attacks cannot cause these physical problems.)

      Yes   No

Are you annoyed that you won't enjoy the exposure?

      Yes   No

Are you convinced that you will fail?

      Yes   No

If you answered yes to any of these, take some time to reflect on your anticipated negative outcomes. Are they the same or different across the various exposures you are scheduling and trying? What other patterns do you notice?

_____

_____

_____

_____

    Any of these anticipated negative outcomes may be a possibility for you. Knowing yours can be useful in exposing yourself to the possibility. More specifically, you may need to pursue your exposure practice with your anticipated negative outcome in mind and test it out. See if you can call its bluff. You will need to stay long enough to know whether you get embarrassed or get hurt or lose control or enjoy the experience in the end. Although there isn't a set time frame for any of these things to happen or not happen, repeated exposure without experiencing the anticipated negative outcome will help to convince you that it's not going to happen (or, similar to Tommy's fears of being scratched, you will learn that it is not that bad even if it does happen).

Another possible explanation is that you selected an exposure that may have been too challenging for you to be able to appreciate the learning and experience a reduction in negative emotions in the moment. Let us return to the analogy of working out to try to explain this process. If you are pushing yourself to run farther or faster, will you necessarily feel less strain during the run itself? If you typically run one mile and are trying to push yourself to complete two miles today, would you expect to start to feel the run become easier at the 1.5 mile mark or 1.9 mile mark? No, you wouldn't. With exposures, you are pushing yourself to stay in a situation that you typically avoid (or quickly escape from). Choosing to stay is associated with increased negative emotions and discomfort. It is likely that the initial negative emotions were intense and did not decrease enough (or fast enough) for you to take notice by the time the exposure ended. As long as the exposure did not end while your negative emotions were actively worsening, you will be fine. If you did leave before your negative emotions plateaued or stabilized, see the upcoming section on leaving an exposure too early.

Now that you've walked away from the exposure, please think back to the experience.

What it as bad as you thought that it would be?

_____

_____

Did the anticipated negative outcome occur?

_____

_____

If so, was it as bad as you expected?

_____

_____

Did you ever think that you'd be able to stay that long?

_____

_____

These types of questions after the exposure can help you to appreciate the learning that occurred during the exposure, even if you didn't feel it in the moment. And if you do feel it, it can help you to feel more confident and experience less-severe negative emotions during your next exposure. You will start to see the cracks in the armor that your avoidance has constructed around you. Please review the model in figure 3.2, Using Exposure to End the Avoidance/Isolation Cycle. Even if your negative emotions did not reduce in your initial exposure, they did plateau or stop worsening, so you were able to learn from the experience. And that learning should make future exposure practices easier in terms of less urge to avoid, less negative emotions, and eventual reductions in the moment.

Possible Outcome #3: You tried some exposures and learned a lot from them (stayed long enough).

With which exposures were you able to push yourself to stay and fight through the negative emotions and learn that it wasn't as bad as you had thought?

_____

_____

_____

This is obviously a great place to be. You completed an exposure, experienced initial negative emotions (peak), and then learned that the anticipated negative outcome did not occur and you felt better (pass) or at least you didn't feel any worse (plateau). This outcome is depicted as the 2a (pass) and 2b (plateau) in figure 3.2, Using Exposure to End the Avoidance/Isolation Cycle. There isn't much to say about this outcome apart from telling you "very well done!" Do you think you were a little lucky because it fell on a good day, or maybe the setting wasn't as busy as it normally is? Sure, there may be several excuses that your negative emotions will use to minimize your success ("you just got lucky"). But those things don't matter. What matters is that you scheduled a challenging exposure, you completed it, *and* you learned from the experience. You showed up, stayed, grappled with the discomfort, and won.

What did you learn? Write down all the insights you gathered.

_____

_____

_____

_____

_____

I hope you learned that it wasn't as difficult as you anticipated. You also probably learned that you can do it again, and that it'll likely go the same way as with this practice (or even get easier and easier). That is the next step of the exposure plan. It is precisely these kinds of exposures—the ones that are difficult, but that you can withstand and learn from—that you should continue. Be sure to schedule repeats of these exposures as well as similar exposures to reinforce the learning and checking off avoided situations from your record. But again, nice job. Great work. Gold star. You are on track. Keep it up, and this treatment is going to be quite successful for you to stop avoiding and start living.

Possible Outcome #4: You tried multiple sets of exposures more than once and learned a lot from them (stayed long enough).

Were there any exposures that you committed to being in repeatedly, for the long haul? What were they?

_____

_____

_____

Why do you think you were able to try these more than once?

_____

_____

_____

This is the only category better than the preceding one. You completed one exposure and stayed long enough to experience negative emotions (peak); you learned that the anticipated negative outcome didn't materialize; you experienced a reduction of negative emotions (pass); and, I hope that you noticed an increase in positive emotions along the way. But above and beyond all that, you also were able to accomplish this pattern on more than one occasion. This pattern is depicted as the 3 and 4 in figure 3.2, Using Exposure to End the Avoidance/Isolation Cycle. This is the *whole purpose* of these exposure practices. I'm impressed that you've gotten here already. At the same time, I know that you still have a ways to go to reach your treatment goals. You may cross out or check off this exposure on your Record of Avoided Situations Worksheet. Now replace it with a harder version (busier store, longer walk, larger social gathering), if you still have room to go. It is not over yet, but it is likely that your world should start to brighten.

If you experienced this last outcome, you will need to continue scheduling and performing exposures at a slightly more difficult level. List a few ways that you can increase your challenge this next week:

_____

_____

_____

Or, if completing the exposures has allowed you to reach one of your treatment goals, check it off your list and prepare yourself for the next set of exposures associated with your next treatment goal. Of course, I'm excited and congratulate you on this accomplishment. Very well done! Great job! Total rock star! However, the best reward for this experience will not be coming from me. It will be your internal feelings associated with this success, your knowledge of what you accomplished through exposures, as well as the potential acknowledgment from your family, friends, coworkers, or neighbors who see the difficult changes that you are making. You are becoming the hero of your story.

Possible Outcome #5: You tried some exposures and did not learn from them (left too early).

Did you leave any exposures in increasing discomfort? If so, when did that happen?

_____

_____

_____

This is totally okay at this stage in treatment, as well as understandable. This is one of the most common outcomes at this point. You scheduled your exposure practice and went into it with the best intentions. However, you just couldn't stay in the situation long enough to learn anything other than what you knew already: "this sucks." It's the same reaction that you had going into this treatment. Now, it is the same feeling after four chapters of this book.

Well, do not get discouraged. No one said this would be easy—at any rate, I definitely didn't. There is good news and bad news associated with this outcome.

Let's start with the bad news. When you leave an exposure before you learn about your anticipated negative outcome, you are reinforcing your avoidance and isolation, with their short-term benefits. When you left, you felt better. It's the same old trick that avoidance has been using since this all started. Just keep in mind that you are working through this treatment to stop the long-term negatives and start living. You will get there. You just need to keep pushing yourself.

Next time, try to incorporate the "one more minute" technique described in week 4. Or, alternatively, set a total time limit going into the exposure. If you made it for twenty minutes on your first attempt, set your targeted departure at thirty minutes. If that still isn't long enough to prove that your anticipated negative outcome is not going to happen, set your next targeted departure time at forty minutes. With each delay in leaving, you will get closer and closer to experiencing the plateau in your negative emotions and learning that the anticipated negative outcome did not happen (or that it wasn't as bad as you expected it to be). Eventually, your avoidance will turn tail and start avoiding you.

Okay. So the bad news wasn't exactly that bad. Now let's turn to the good news. The good news concerns what you *chose* to do differently. This situation did not happen because you had to do it, or because someone forced you to do it (or at least it shouldn't have happened for those reasons, per the Exposure Rules in week 4). This exposure happened because you were ready to challenge your avoidance and isolation and related negative emotions. You decided that it was time to fight back. That is very good news.

For how long have you simply accepted your situation (days, weeks, months, years)?

_____

For how long have you been avoiding the situation that you attempted in your exposure (days, weeks, months, years)?

_____

Your decision to fight back after all this time is something to be proud of. It represents a large step forward, even if it doesn't feel that way. But again, one large step is just the beginning. You're going to forge ahead, following this attempt with many more, each step larger (and longer in duration) until you find out what is at the end (did your anticipated negative outcome occur?) and you are ready to apply that learning to more and more situations on your journey to stop avoiding and start living.

Possible Outcome #6: You tried some exposures, but you did not try others.

Was there anything that you just avoided completely? Which exposures did you pass on because you felt total emotional resistance?

_____

_____

_____

If this happened, I hope it was with only a couple of your scheduled exposures. If so, that is completely fine. Again, you purposely scheduled a lot of exposures, knowing that you wouldn't complete 100 percent of them. From Mark's example in the previous chapter, he completed only half of his exposures and still demonstrated significant improvements in challenging his avoidance and isolation and related negative emotions. Assuming that you were able to complete other exposures that fell into the previous categories, you will be fine too. Those exposures are the drivers of change. But we still need to investigate why you felt unable to complete these exposures and refine your future exposure practices accordingly.

Although there may be countless reasons for not being able to complete some of your exposures (weather, scheduling conflict, car problems, illness), there is one reason that merits extra discussion.

Did you avoid the exposure practice because you felt that it was too hard?

    Yes   No

If you answered yes, know that this is a common response early in treatment as well. You haven't had the benefit of learning from successful exposure practices and the added confidence that gives you. That will come in time. Until you get there, my best recommendation is to simply keep scheduling and trying to *try* them. Of course, you could dial back the difficulty level or type of situation selected, but I'll argue that it's too early to do that. Right now you should be trying everything. Break down the walls that your avoidance has created around these situations, and stop listening to its tricks. Do not reinforce them by labeling something too difficult. If you continue to be unable to approach a specific exposure or two after another chapter or two, we will address that then. For now, just keep pushing.

Possible Outcome #7: You did not complete any exposure exercises.

This is the section I really hope you won't need to read. On the one hand, it's great that you are still reading, despite a lot of frustration and probably a little hopelessness. You haven't given up yet, and that is something to take pride in.

There are a few reasons why you may be here. Perhaps…

- Did you select exposures that were simply too hard across the board?

- Are you are not convinced that this treatment approach will work for you?

- Did you just not feel like doing it?

Whatever the reason, my response is going to be the same. Your villain (avoidance) is still winning, but it does not have to stay that way. You don't have to keep avoiding and feeling terrible and overwhelmed by negative emotions. But rather than trying to motivate you here by listing all of the reasons for picking up your sword (exposure) and starting this critical change, I think that it is best for you to return to:

- Your stated reasons for making this change, in week 2

- The model for Using Exposure to End the Avoidance/Isolation Cycle, figure 3.2

- The Exposure Rules, in week 4

Once you've completed those reviews, take a mulligan and retry the exposures that you planned in your exposure monitoring form in week 4. Do the Sunday exposures planned for last Sunday on next Sunday. Do last Monday's scheduled exposures on next Monday. And so on. You are still reading. You haven't given up yet. Go out there and fight your avoidance and isolation.

SCHEDULING YOUR NEXT EXPOSURES

As soon as you have two weeks of exposures under your belt, it is time to plan your next set of exposures in your fight to overcome avoidance. Ideally, some of the exposures that you tried have worked well and led to new learning, while others have worked less well. Regardless of the specific outcomes, you have learned from each experience and developed new refinements to improve the likelihood of success going forward. You are learning to be better and better at challenging your avoidance.

You may find it helpful to quickly reference your Record of Avoided Situations, treatment goals, and exposure rules. Also, review your progress as recorded on last week's Exposure Tracking Worksheet. Use it as a guide as you choose where to increase the difficulty and to repeat exposures for additional learning. And again, revisiting the previous examples in week 4, be sure to schedule a lot of exposures and schedule on specific days and times to improve your chances at continued success.

Please use the worksheet that follows to schedule your exposures. Copies of this worksheet are available for download at http://www.newharbinger.com/45663.

Exposure Tracking Worksheet

	Planned Exposure	Scheduled Day/Time	Initial Symptoms (–100 to +100)	Peak Symptoms (–100 to +100)	Final Symptoms (–100 to +100)	Total Time
Example	Shop at grocery store	Tuesday @ 2 p.m.	–50	–80	–40	45min
1						
2						
3						
4						
5						
6						
7						
8						

Planned Exposure	Scheduled Day/Time	Initial Symptoms (−100 to +100)	Peak Symptoms (−100 to +100)	Final Symptoms (−100 to +100)	Total Time
9					
10					
11					
12					
13					
14					
15					
16					
17					
18					

Now that your exposures are planned, it's that time again— to make sure that you don't forget what you have planned. Make a ton of copies and post them all over your home, work, and car. Proudly brag (or complain) to your friends and family about your planned activities. In fact, plan the activities with your friends and family to feel even more obligated to *try* the exposures (as long as they aren't used as safety behaviors). And program the exposures into your phone with alarms and reminders. You will not forget these, and you will take another step forward in challenging your avoidance and negative emotions through exposures. Be the hero of this story and continue your hunt for the villains (avoidance and isolation) to win the day (overcome negative emotions) and celebrate your victory (experience positive emotions). It is time to build on your initial progress and get closer to your treatment goals.

WRAPPING UP

This chapter was all about your exposure exercises. In fact, nearly every chapter going forward is going to be all about your exposure exercises. They simply are that important to your symptom improvement and the attainment of your treatment goals. After assessing your symptoms, we categorized your exposure practices to reinforce the successes and problem solve the continued challenges. We will be repeating this process each week until your Record of Avoided Situations is a thing of the past and your treatment goals are all checked off. This may seem like a stretch, but I bet that it no longer seems impossible. You have learned a powerful tool and how to use it effectively. Now, it comes down to time (and a lot of practice) to get you where you want to be.

In the next chapter, I will introduce a way to separate your exposures into four new categories: situational, physical/interoceptive, thought/imaginal, and positive emotional. This new way to approach exposures likely will open your eyes to additional avoidance in your life and potential areas of improvement. Fortunately, exposure will work for those areas too, with just a little bit of further refinement. Don't worry; together, we will get you to meet or exceed each of your treatment goals along your journey to stop avoiding and start living.

Overcome the Four Types of Avoidance

You have completed the first five weeks of standing up to avoidance and isolation. Treatment progress should be coming soon, if it hasn't already begun to show itself. In this chapter, we are going to continue to follow the same pattern. We will start by assessing your symptoms and treatment progress; and we will review your exposure practices (referencing the categories from the previous chapter). Then we will shift to incorporating new content to help you refine your exposure practices by diving deeper into avoidance. More specifically, we will be sorting your avoidance patterns into the four categories—situational avoidance, physical avoidance, thought avoidance, and positive emotional avoidance—and you'll learn how to differentiate them from each other.

The good news is that your progress to this point has allowed you to embark on this next stage in treatment. Now you need to make sure that you flesh out all of the specific kinds of avoidance contributing to your negative emotions, and then apply slightly specialized exposures to target each. Let's keep up the fight.

REFLECTING ON THE LAST CHAPTER AND PREPARING TO MOVE DEEPER

It's time once again to complete and score your Symptom Checklist and enter your score and today's date in the Appendix 1 Symptom Tracking Form. This will be your fourth score now. Hopefully you should start seeing a change or pattern of changes in your scores.

Symptom Checklist	Not at all	A little	Moderately	Very much so
1. Depressed mood, most of the day, nearly every day	0	1	2	3
2. Avoidance of people, places, and situations (e.g., crowds)	0	1	2	3
3. Feeling constantly on guard and preparing for danger (e.g., back to the wall)	0	1	2	3
4. Frequent periods of intense anxiety or panic	0	1	2	3
5. Avoidance of physical sensations (e.g., heart racing, heavy breathing)	0	1	2	3
6. Avoidance of unpleasant thoughts or memories (e.g., of a car accident)	0	1	2	3
7. Loss of interest or pleasure, most of the day, nearly every day	0	1	2	3
8. Avoidance of activities that were previously enjoyed (e.g., working out)	0	1	2	3
Total Score:				
Date:				

How did you do? Did your score change since your earlier scores? Looking back at forms you filled out a few weeks ago, can you see a pattern starting to develop in your scores? There are several possible outcomes here that we should discuss. Check the one that best describes your scores:

☐ Consistent Pattern of No Change (or Symptom Worsening)

☐ Inconsistent Pattern of Ups and Downs

☐ Consistent Pattern of Symptom Improvement

Pattern #1: Consistent Pattern of No Change (or Symptom Worsening)

You are five chapters into the treatment now, with the most recent ones all dedicated to exposure practices. The lack of change at this point is a little surprising, but not a reason to give up yet either. One explanation for this type of lack of change is related to your success with the exposure practices. It is possible that these have yet to cause significant improvements in your symptoms. Remember our workout analogy? It can take weeks of working out at the gym before you see improvements to your physical health, strength, and stamina. And each of us responds differently to exercise, depending on our starting condition and body type. Exposures are no different. It may take weeks of practice for exposures to affect your longstanding patterns of avoidance and negative emotions. Another possibility is that your engagement in exposures is still insufficient to lead to change. As detailed in the Exposure Rules, exposures must be completed frequently and for a long enough duration to learn from the experience. If you are practicing exposures only a couple of times a week or only for a few minutes, they are unlikely to result in many improvements at this point. Similarly, sometimes individuals complete exposures only as part of their normal routine, rather than as stand-alone practices specifically completed to challenge avoidance. For example, someone may go to the store (because they have to do their usual unavoidable weekly shopping, rather than making a specific trip focused on exposure) and stay only as long as the shopping takes to complete (rather than staying long enough to learn from the experience). This approach is unlikely to be much different from what you were already doing before starting this book, so it stands to reason that it won't generate much change. From the working out perspective, would you expect that your required brief daily walk from the parking lot to your office or your occasionally helping a friend move would lead to sudden improvements to your physical health? Finally, you may be being too hard on yourself with your self-ratings. If you're not expecting changes, you may not notice them either and continue to circle the same scores. Whatever the reason—whether it's one of these possibilities or a reason not mentioned—the solution is going to be the same. You need to continue to push yourself to complete sufficiently long exposures on a regular basis. Keep up with the exposures, keep challenging your avoidance, and you'll eventually start seeing changes in your world and your outlook. You can do this.

Are there any things that you should change about your exposures going forward to encourage symptom improvement (see the Exposure Rules for ways to improve your exposures)?

_____

_____

_____

Pattern #2: Inconsistent Ups and Downs

This is the most common pattern of findings at this point in treatment. You are having your good weeks and your less-good weeks, depending in part on the success of your exposure practices and weekly stressors. In weeks when exposures were successful, I would expect a reduction in your avoidance and negative emotions. However, you shouldn't necessarily expect that to happen every week. Rather, expect that life may get in the way early in treatment and lead you to mixed efforts and successes in your practices. If you joined a gym for the first time in years, you wouldn't expect to succeed in getting to the gym every time you planned to, or to achieve a trajectory of steadily more difficult workouts. It would take time to develop that routine, with some weeks easier than others. The same is true for exposures. However, I expect that will start changing now, for several reasons. First, routines, whether they be working out or completing exposures, become easier with time. The more that you practice them, the easier it'll become to continue to practice them. Second, your exposure should start becoming more effective at reducing your negative emotions and improving your positive emotions. And third, we are not done yet. I still have several ways to improve your exposures and learn to use additional skills (non-exposure techniques). You are on your way. Keep it up.

Did anything strike you in the pattern just described? Are there any things that you should change going forward to encourage symptom improvement (see the Exposure Rules)?

_____

_____

_____

Pattern #3: Consistent Improvement

Well, this definitely is a good place to be. As in previous chapters, you wouldn't necessarily expect to be here at this point in treatment. That is all the more reason for my enthusiasm. You have attempted your first couple of sets of exposure practices and (most likely) experienced many early successes in challenging your avoidance and have been feeling better during these last few weeks. Keep up the momentum by continuing to work the program as you push toward your goals. You are on your way to finishing your story with a "happily ever after." Now take a moment to look back at your treatment goals (week 2). Let's see how you are doing.

Have you completed any of your treatment goals through observable change?

_____

_____

_____

Which goals have you not reached yet?

_____

_____

_____

Regardless of whether you have reached each of your originally listed treatment goals or not (or are still just getting started in your treatment progress), it's important to review them again to determine whether you've made all of the gains that are needed. Now that you've been on your journey to overcome avoidance for some time, are there other treatment goals that could be added to your list? Are there other areas that you think you can change now?

_____

_____

_____

_____

If you are able to identify more treatment goals, return to your original list to add them, or download and print another online copy from http://www.newharbinger.com/45663.

REVIEWING YOUR EXPOSURE PRACTICE

In the previous chapter, you assigned yourself a set of exposure practices. This was your second week standing up to avoidance. You scheduled each of those exposures for a specific day and time, and with a targeted goal and motivation in mind for challenging yourself.

So how did it go? Describe your overall experience, writing down the most important elements.

_____

_____

_____

In the previous chapter, we went through the most common outcomes for your exposure practices. Rather than repeating them here, categorize your exposure outcomes and then refer to the outcome discussion in the previous chapter to better understand your progress and how to plan your next set of exposures.

Outcome #1: You tried some exposures and did not experience negative emotions. Check this outcome in week 5 for ways to improve your exposures this week. What are some reasons why your practice may have gone this way?

_____

_____

Outcome #2: You tried some exposures and learned a little from them (almost stayed long enough). See week 5 for ways to improve your exposures this week. What are some reasons why your practice may have gone this way?

_____

_____

Outcome #3: You tried some exposures and learned a lot from them (stayed long enough). See week 5. What are some reasons why your practice may have gone this way?

_____

_____

Outcome #4: You tried multiple sets of exposures more than once and learned a lot from them (stayed long enough). See week 5. What are some reasons why your practice may have gone this way?

_____

_____

Outcome #5: You tried some exposures and did not learn from them (left too early). See week 5 for ways to improve your exposures this week. What are some reasons why your practice may have gone this way?

_____

_____

Outcome #6: You tried some exposures, but you did not try others. See week 5 for ways to improve your exposures this week. What are some reasons why your practice may have gone this way?

_____

_____

Outcome #7: You did not complete any exposure exercises. See week 5 for ways to repeat and improve your planned exposures this week. What are some reasons why your practice may have gone this way?

_____

_____

I hope this categorization exercise has helped you understand where to place your focus for future exposure practices. As you establish a workout routine, it is unlikely that all parts of your body will respond to exercises at the same pace. For example, would you expect your biceps (arms) and quadriceps (legs) to strengthen at the same rate? Would you be able to lift the same weight with your biceps and quadriceps or complete the same number of repetitions? The simple answer is no. And the same is true for your exposures. Don't expect to respond at the same rate or speed to exposures ranging from heavy traffic, to large crowds and kids' sporting events, to social gatherings with coworkers or date nights with your spouse. Understanding these differences should allow for better planning and targeting of your avoidance as you continue your journey.

THE MANY FACES OF AVOIDANCE

Up to this point, you have been learning precisely how avoidance influences your negative emotions by showing up week after week in our exposure practices. I hope you have had many victories thus far, with many more to come. However, as with any good story, there are a few final tricks that avoidance will try to turn the tables and keep its grip on your life. Avoidance is not just one behavioral trap getting in the way of your life; it can be one of four different presentations. Yes, there are four different types of avoidance that you may need to challenge. The good news is that you already have the tool that you need to overcome any of the four, and you may have even challenged more than one of the types of avoidance without realizing it. Let's get to know the four types of avoidance.

Situational Avoidance

Situational avoidance is the most common type of avoidance, and it was used in most of the examples you've seen here so far. In situational avoidance, you avoid people, places, things, and situations because interacting with them generates negative emotions such as fear, anxiety, anger, depression, and worry. In week 3, Tommy's avoidance of cats presents an example of situational avoidance. To be brief, Tommy avoided cats because he felt intense fear and anxiety when he came into contact with them. You've most likely been wrestling with this kind of avoidance all along.

Can you think of any of your avoided activities that fall into the category of situational avoidance? Please list them here.

_____

_____

_____

Physical Avoidance

Physical avoidance is a little different from situational avoidance. It functions in much the same fashion in terms of situations being avoided because they increase negative emotions such as fear and anxiety, but it is not the situation itself that exacerbates the negative emotions, but the physical symptoms associated with the situation. For example, someone experiencing physical avoidance may avoid walking up a flight of stairs because it causes their heart rate to spike, or avoid attending a funny movie because laughing causes rapid breathing, or avoid swimming because it restricts breathing. Each of these avoided situations are most commonly associated with a fear of experiencing a panic attack and the associated feared consequences of a panic attack such as a heart attack. (I hope you recall my assurances that panic attacks cannot cause heart attacks, losing control, or going crazy). However, physical avoidance may persist unless you commit to facing it head on with slightly modified exposures we will be practicing.

Kelly's Story

Kelly was a thirty-two-year-old woman I treated in Southern Ontario. Kelly was working a new job and enjoying it thus far. She woke up each morning, helped her kids off to school, and headed into the office. She had worked in the same banking industry for years but had finally moved from the small bank branch to the regional office. Kelly looked forward to going to work, and she liked her coworkers. Oddly, though, Kelly started to experience panic symptoms (sweating, racing heart, rapid breathing, and dizziness) upon arriving at work each day. She would excuse herself to the bathroom to take deep breaths and splash water on her face (mild avoidance). Over time, the avoidance cycle started to win the day, and Kelly would end up leaving work to avoid her physical symptoms and the associated fear of having a heart attack. By the time that

I met Kelly, she was on temporary disability from work due to her severe anxiety and physical avoidance.

SEARCHING FOR PHYSICAL AVOIDANCE IN YOUR WORLD

Kelly's story may have sounded very familiar to you, or maybe it did not. Physical avoidance is most common in individuals who experience panic attacks or strong social fears (the physical symptoms may include facial flushing, sweaty palms, dry throat with a "lump" that impedes talking). Either way, there is a set of physical challenge exercises that will help you to identify whether physical avoidance is a part of your story.

These exercises are designed to elicit negative emotions in individuals with physical avoidance. Please try each and note whether it causes both physical symptoms *and* negative emotions (fear, anxiety, or anger).

1. Jog in place fast enough to speed up your heart rate and breathing (60 seconds).

2. Hold your breath for as long as you can.

3. Shake your head from side to side in the classic "no" motion (30 seconds).

4. Breathe rapidly and shallowly (hyperventilate) (60 seconds).

5. Pinch your nose closed and breathe only through a small coffee-stirring straw (120 seconds).

6. Spin in place (to be safe, do this in a carpeted space near cushioned furniture) (10 seconds).

7. Sit with your head down between your knees for 30 seconds, and then straighten up quickly.

Which, if any, of these exercises caused you distressing physical sensations and negative emotions?

_____

_____

What negative emotions did the exercise(s) trigger?

_____

_____

Thought Avoidance

This kind of avoidance may be trickier than the others. Rather than manifesting through your avoiding situations, thought avoidance primarily occurs inside your head. It involves avoiding difficult or traumatic memories or reoccurring thought patterns because they bring about negative emotions (anxiety, fear, worry, sadness, numbing, anger). These avoided memories could be the sudden and unexpected death of a loved one, a violent car accident, a physical or sexual assault, a violent crime, a natural disaster, a combat deployment, a severe injury, or any number of other past events. It is normal to have negative emotions associated with these types of memories. I would expect you to feel sadness when thinking about your grandmother's sudden heart attack or nervousness when recalling the time that you were mugged at gunpoint. The difference with thought avoidance is the person's overwhelming efforts to avoid thinking or talking about the event(s) at all costs. And of course, avoiding one's thoughts is not an easy thing to do, as you will see in the following example.

Earl's Story

Earl was a seventy-two-year-old Vietnam veteran living in Coastal South Carolina. Earl was retired and living with his wife of over forty years. Together, they had raised their children to adulthood; like many older adults, they were now helping to raise their grandchildren. Although Earl had served his country in Vietnam in the late 1960s, he never spoke about the war. In fact, Earl's family didn't even know that he ever served in the U.S. Army. His family knew that he didn't like to watch war movies and would turn off the news whenever they covered any global conflicts, and that he would need some time to himself after accidentally catching the wrong program on television. His family just thought that Earl was very emotional when it came to war. And he was, but Earl's intense sadness and anxiety stemmed from his service and the events that took place during his deployment to Vietnam. There, Earl's company was ambushed by the enemy, Earl was injured, and his best friend, Douglas, was killed.

Ever since, Earl has done his best to try not to think about it. However, that in itself is much easier said than done. How can you avoid your own thoughts? For example, if I instruct you to not think about a pink elephant, how well are you able to avoid thinking about it? Earl was having the same problem. It all came to a head when Earl unexpectedly received a Purple Heart in the mail, awarded to those who sustained wartime injuries at the hands of the enemy. Despite his never wanting the acknowledgment, a local veterans organization had requested it on his behalf after completing a research project on the conflict. Earl's secret was out of the bag, and his thought avoidance and negative emotions took over.

Can you think of any of your avoidance that falls into the category of thought avoidance? Have you experienced any past events (or some other painful memory) that you continue to struggle with and would prefer not to remember or think about? Please list them here.

_____

_____

_____

Positive Emotional Avoidance

The fourth and final type is *positive emotional avoidance*. This type of avoidance differs from the first three in one significant way: although the avoided situations may look the same (stores, sporting events, get-togethers with friends and family, movie theaters), these situations are avoided due not to an increase of negative emotions (fear, anxiety, sadness, anger), but rather to a *lack of positive emotions* (lack of interest, feeling numb or detached, lack of motivation or drive). Put differently, individuals with positive emotional avoidance decline to participate in activities because they feel like they either will not enjoy them or do not deserve to enjoy them due to long-standing feelings of worthlessness. And so, they simply decide to stay home and miss out, leading to fewer experiences of positive emotions (less enjoyment) and eventual development of negative emotions (sadness, loneliness, despair, numbing).

Patricia's Story

Patricia, age forty-three, lived in Eastern Massachusetts. Patricia had grown up in the area and decided to stay through adulthood, so she was surrounded by family and friends. In fact, she lived in the same neighborhood as her parents and siblings. Patricia worked a demanding office job with no shortage of stressors. Although there wasn't an obvious start to her behavior, Patricia began to pull away from all of her usual activities. It started with her missing the occasional game of her nephew's soccer team, or church service on Sunday morning. Although Patricia usually would tell her affected family or friends that she was feeling under the weather or that she had to catch up on work, the truth was Patricia simply didn't want to go to these events anymore. She didn't think that she would enjoy herself, and she decided to just stay home and do nothing in particular. Over time, her positive emotional avoidance took over and she missed more and more activities, eventually leading to missed days of work, frequent periods of isolation and loneliness, and significant symptoms of depression.

Can you think of any of your avoided activities that fall into the category of positive emotional avoidance? Please list them here.

_____

_____

_____

KEEPING TABS ON ALL FOUR

The next step is to identify and separate your remaining avoided activities into the four types of avoidance so you can better understand of the types of avoidance that you engage in, as well as develop additional exposure skills to challenge your avoidance. This is the first part of the two-part process. At first, you are learning about the four types of avoidance. After that we'll discuss ways to adjust your exposure practices for each of the avoidance types. You still will be using the same method, but learning to wield it a little differently for each specific type of avoidance you might have in order to better take advantage of your motivation to change and reach your treatment goals.

Refer back to your answers for each of the four types of avoidance, as well as the remaining items on your Record of Avoided Situations, and enter them into the four categories in this new Record of Avoidance. Additional copies of this form can be printed from http://www.newharbin ger.com/45663. It is not required that you have items for all four types of avoidance. Your answers will depend on your experience of negative and positive emotions and related use of avoidance.

Record of Avoidance

Please record any people, place, thing, task, activity, and/or thought or memory that you have avoided due to negative emotions or a lack of positive emotions. These might include shopping at certain stores (situational), completing certain activities that cause physical sensations (physical), thinking or talking about certain past events (thought), or completing certain activities that you used to enjoy (positive emotional). Ratings could be negative emotions (–100 to 0) or for lack of positive emotions (0 to +100), with –100 as the most severe negative emotions, 0 as completely neutral, and +100 as the most positive emotions.

Situational Avoidance		Physical Avoidance		Thought Avoidance		Positive Emotional Avoidance	
Situation	Rating	Situation	Rating	Thought/Memory	Rating	Situation	Rating
1.		1.		1.		1.	
2.		2.		2.		2.	
3.		3.		3.		3.	
4.		4.		4.		4.	
5.		5.		5.		5.	
6.		6.		6.		6.	
7.		7.		7.		7.	
8.		8.		8.		8.	
9.		9.		9.		9.	
10.		10.		10.		10.	
11.		11.		11.		11.	
12.		12.		12.		12.	

When you look at your avoidance practices separated into categories this way, what do you notice? Do you have more avoidance in one category than in another?

_____

_____

_____

_____

_____

PLANNING NEXT WEEK'S EXPOSURES

You have three weeks of exposures under your belt now, and guess what: we are going to do another week of them. By now, some of your exposures have worked well and led to new learning, while others have worked less well. You have applied problem-solving strategies and become better at hanging in there when the discomfort gets intense. You might be thinking that addressing different types of avoidance cannot be that different from what you've been doing for all of these weeks. Well, in a way, you would be correct.

You already know how to do exposures. You've worked on them for weeks and (hopefully) worked to perfect your practices over time, with progressively increasing successes week after week. And these new exposures for physical avoidance, thought avoidance, and positive emotional avoidance are not terribly different from what you have been doing for all of these weeks. However, there are differences, and they could be important as you work to stop avoiding and start living again. Let's go through the four types quickly to see the important differences to keep in mind as you plan next week's exposures.

Situational Exposures

Situational avoidance, the most common type of avoidance, has been used as the primary example throughout the text to this point. It leads people to avoid other people, places, things, and situations because it causes negative emotions such as fear, anxiety, anger, depression, and worry. The story of Tommy and his avoidance of cats was an example of situational avoidance.

The way that Tommy used exposure to overcome his avoidance was an example of situational exposures. As such, the Exposure Rules you learned in week 4 will remain unchanged for any situational exposures. The skills that you've practiced to this point are well-suited to overcome situational avoidance. Keep it up.

Physical Exposures

Physical avoidance occurs when situations are avoided due to the connection between physical sensations (heart racing, rapid breathing, dizziness) and negative emotions (fear, anxiety, and anger). We discussed the patient example of Kelly, who ended up on temporary disability due to experiencing panic attacks at work and being unable to remain in the office as a result. If you identified physical avoidance during the tests provided earlier and listed any exercises in your expanded Record of Avoidance, keep reading to learn how to tailor your exposures accordingly. If you did not identify any physical avoidance, feel free to skip ahead to the next section for thought avoidance.

Physical exposures largely work the same way as standard exposures (or situational exposures). Rather than a store, movie theater, or social gathering (as in situational exposures), the targets in physical exposures are the physical sensations themselves. Thinking back to Kelly's example, she would arrive at work and feel a rush of physical symptoms and related negative emotions (fear of having a heart attack).

What do you think would happen if she stayed at work long enough to test her anticipated negative outcome? What would happen if her physical sensations became intense?

_____

_____

_____

The goal with physical exposures is to answer those very questions.

Kelly's Story (continued)

When Kelly arrived to treatment, she was on temporary disability after the repeated onset of strong physical sensations caused her to leave work daily (physical avoidance). When approaching treatment, Kelly focused on physical exposures (exposures to heart racing and dizziness) rather than situational exposures (exposures to going to work), because her negative emotions were most related to physical sensations themselves. Kelly was not anxious or fearful of her job; in fact, she really enjoyed it. Rather, Kelly was anxious and fearful of the strong physical sensations that she experienced when going to work (fear of having a heart attack). And so, Kelly completed the physical avoidance challenge exercises and planned her exposures accordingly. She repeatedly walked up flights of stairs and jogged in place to get her heart rate and breathing to increase. She also completed periods of spinning in place to cause dizziness. The goal for these exposures is to break the connection between physical sensations and negative emotions, by completing the exposure and learning the consequences. Kelly had learned that panic attacks are not physically dangerous, but she needed to prove it to herself. Despite no changes in her physical sensations after repeated physical challenges (her heart always raced if she jogged up enough stairs), Kelly's negative emotions began to reduce in severity (as shown in figure 6.1), leading to reduced physical avoidance, and she was able to return to work without fear of future panic attacks.

Figure 6.1. Reduction of Symptom Severity Through Physical Exposures

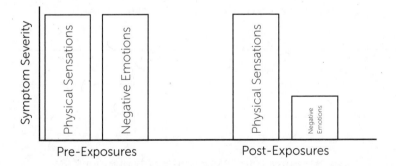

Now it's time to review your results of the physical avoidance challenge exercises and the related activities listed in your expanded Record of Avoidance.

Which physical exposures should be added to your exposure tracking form?

_____

_____

_____

Please keep in mind that these activities differ only in the target of the exposure itself (physical sensations rather than specific situations). Relatedly, one advantage of these exposures is that they can be practiced in sets. Rather than going to a store two or three times weekly for thirty-minute periods, you can walk up and down a flight of stairs for five minutes, stop and learn from the outcome (nothing bad happened), and then repeat for another five-minutes period or increase it to ten minutes, further challenging your physical avoidance. You should schedule these exposures in blocks (for example, three sets of spinning in place for thirty seconds each). Over time, you too will break the connection between your physical sensations and your negative emotions.

Thought Avoidance

Thought avoidance occurs when traumatic or highly unpleasant thoughts or memories are avoided due to the connection with negative emotions (fear, anxiety, and anger). We discussed the patient example of Earl, the Vietnam veteran who was surprised by a Purple Heart in the mail and was overwhelmed with traumatic memories of his unit being ambushed and his friend Douglas's death. If you did not identify any thought avoidance, you can skip ahead to the next section for positive emotional avoidance.

Thought exposures largely work in the same way as regular exposures (situational exposures). However, in comparison to situational avoidance (in which, for example, you simply don't go to stores) or physical avoidance (in which you try to stay calm and avoid physical activity), can you avoid your own thoughts? The unfortunate answer is *no*. I expect that that answer may surprise you. Maybe you think that you are good at avoiding your highly unpleasant or traumatic memories. Maybe you think that you just need to avoid triggers (violent movies, loud noises, or the evening news) and you won't think of them. Or maybe you think that you are really good at distracting yourself once your memories have been triggered, as long as you can have time to yourself (thought avoidance causing situational avoidance).

But as hard as you may try, you simply cannot avoid your thoughts. And the harder that you try, the more you will think about your highly unpleasant or traumatic memories and the more negative emotions you will experience. And so, if avoiding them does not work, your only choice is to embrace your memories until they no longer cause intense negative emotions.

That probably sounds strange to you right now. I expect that you may feel some doubt that they can be effective for your highly unpleasant or traumatic memory. Before returning to Earl's story, let's turn to the example of Alex and his reaction to coping with the emotions and memories associated with his grandfather's unexpected passing.

Alex's Story: The Power of a Funeral

There are many examples of highly unpleasant or traumatic memories to choose from. But the sudden and unexpected death of a loved one is one of the few that tends to have a built-in coping strategy: to embrace your memories and move forward. Unlike the previous examples, Alex is not one of my former patients. Alex is more like Tommy (who fears cats) in that he could be anyone. Alex is a twenty-four-year-old recent college graduate, living on his own for the first time. One day Alex receives an unexpected early morning call from his mom. His mom explains that his grandfather had a heart attack sometime in the night and passed away. Although Alex's grandmother had died earlier in the year after a long battle with cancer, Alex's grandfather was healthy and active. Alex was devastated by the news and overrun with negative emotions. He had lived with his grandparents throughout college and only recently moved away. He felt that he should have been there for his grandfather and that if he had been, he could have prevented his death. Alex began to try to distract himself from these feelings and avoid thinking about his grandfather (thought avoidance) and pull himself away from painful reminders. He called off work to avoid coworkers' condolences; he stopped answering his family's calls, and he hid pictures of his grandparents previously displayed in his apartment. He also avoided his normal activities, such going to the gym or attending his weekly trivia night with friends (thought avoidance leading to situational avoidance).

However, despite the cycle of negative emotions and avoidance pulling him downward, Alex's parents forced him to attend his grandfather's funeral and assist with managing his grandfather's belongings. This process is essentially thought exposure. Alex had to expose himself to his memories of his grandfather's death over and over throughout the weekend. He had to talk to family members and family friends about his grandfather. Alex had to talk about his grandfather's health and the surprise associated with his untimely passing, as well as talk about his grandmother's fight with cancer and her death's effect on his grandfather. The experience was very difficult and filled with many tears. However, as story after story was told, Alex became better able to cope, and he began to share the good stories too (having weekly Sunday dinner with his grandparents during college, his grandparents' surprise when he asked to live with them, and the family trip to the Grand Canyon). By confronting his thought avoidance through thought exposures (repeatedly talking about his grandfather's passing), Alex was able to grieve and heal from his loss. While his grandfather's death would never be a good memory, in time Alex was able to talk about both the good (Sunday dinner) and the bad (heart attack) associated with his grandfather without experiencing overwhelming negative emotions (and the related urge to avoid).

Okay, we have discussed how thought exposures can be similar to a funeral, in that confronting the bad memories can lead to grieving and healing. However, I expect that you may have some doubt that they can be effective for your highly unpleasant or traumatic memories. Let's return to Earl's story and see how they were applied to his traumatic memories.

Earl's Story (continued)

When Earl first arrived to treatment, his attempted thought avoidance had taken over, caused intense negative emotions (fear, anxiety, guilt, depression, and anger), and led to growing situational avoidance (staying in his bedroom all day, missing dinner with his wife, and skipping weekly gatherings with his friends). And Earl was trying his best to forget his traumatic memories, which only made him think about them constantly (the more you try to not think of a pink elephant, the more you think about it). Earl was even having nightmares about the traumatic memory. Not even his sleep was safe from thought avoidance and negative emotions.

Earl was presented with the rationale for thought exposures (Alex's funeral example) and agreed to give them a try. He needed to rejoin his family and friends for their weekly activities (treatment goals) and stop letting them all down (treatment motivation). Thought exposures involved Earl telling the story of his traumatic memory as if he were a master novelist or award-winning movie director. Earl described the scene with each of his senses (touch, smell, taste, hearing, sight) using the first person present tense ("I am pushing my way through the bush while walking through ankle-high water, with rain hitting my pack"). This exposure covers the entire scene, including the really hard parts (Earl's injury and Douglas's death), despite Earl's urges to avoid any experience of intense negative emotions. However, as the exposure model predicts, Earl's negative emotions were reduced as he repeatedly practiced his thought exposures (listening to recordings of his telling of the traumatic event or rereading written narrative of the trauma). Eventually, Earl progressed to telling his wife of the events, and later told his children and close friends. In fact, the family took a trip together to Washington, DC, to make a rubbing of Douglas's name on the Vietnam War Memorial. It was a very emotional experience for them all. Similar to the funeral example, Earl's injury and Douglas's death never become good memories; rather, they remain terrible memories. However, through thought exposures, the memories stopped controlling Earl's actions in terms of thought avoidance, nightmares, and related situational avoidance (he was able to resume watching the nightly news); exposures reduced his negative emotions and allowed the return of positive emotions.

Now it's time to review your expanded Record of Avoidance. Which thought exposures should be added to your exposure tracking form?

_____

_____

_____

_____

How will you repeat the thought exposure?

☐ Record and repeatedly listen to a voice recording of the memory on your smartphone or computer.

☐ Write out and repeatedly reread the narrative.

Please keep in mind that these exposures differ only in the target of the exposure itself (memories rather than a specific situation). Relatedly, one advantage (and associated disadvantage) of these exposures is that they can be practiced anywhere in private. Rather than going to a store two or three times weekly for thirty-minute periods, you can listen to the recording at home or during your lunch break and learn from the outcome (nothing bad happened). However, it is possible that you will practice these exposures and then they will persist in your mind without a change of activity or setting. Try to pair thought exposures with other exposures or activities, especially positive activities (positive emotional exposures scheduled one hour after a thought exposure). Over time, through the use of thought exposures, you too will break the connection between your highly unpleasant or traumatic memories and your negative emotions, on your journey to stop avoiding and start living.

Positive Emotional Exposures

Positive emotional exposures are the fourth and final category of exposures. Rather than being a result of negative emotions, positive emotional avoidance stems from a lack of positive emotions (disinterest, feeling numb or detached, lack of motivation or drive). We discussed the patient example of Patricia, a woman who began to pull away from her friends and family due to reduced interest and enjoyment. I asked you to try to identify any of your avoided activities that fall into the category of positive emotional avoidance. If you did, continue reading to learn how to tailor your exposures accordingly. In fact, even if you didn't, I'd like you to continue reading. Most people, if not everyone, could benefit from added positive and rewarding activities in their life.

Positive emotional exposures work in the same way as regular exposures (situational exposures), with one slight difference. In typical exposures, you attempt to stay in situations long enough to experience negative emotions and allow them to reduce over time and be replaced by positive emotions. In positive emotional exposures, negative emotions typically are very mild (frustration or irritability). So these exposures focus on the second element: increasing positive emotions over time. Put more simply, the goal of positive emotional exposures is to push yourself to participate in activities until you begin to enjoy them again. Does that sound easy? While it may seem fairly straightforward to go do fun activities again, your positive emotional avoidance (and other types of avoidance) has stopped you to this point. And so, it may take a little push to get yourself back to where you need to be.

THINK OF YOUR LIFE LIKE A DINNER MENU

So why aren't you taking part in pleasurable activities like you used to? Are you just in a temporary funk or recovering from an injury or sickness? There may be many reasons, some of which may be explained by our original explanation: the Avoidance/Isolation Model (figure 3.1). Whatever the reason, you need to find a way to build your activities back into your daily routine. To put it more simply, you need to build yourself a better menu.

Well-filled menus are essential for making choices. Please think about the dinner menu at your favorite restaurant. Why do you like it? Which dishes do you want to eat?

_____

_____

If you're like me, my favorite menus are those that offer plenty of enticing options. No matter my mood or appetite, there always are several options that appeal to me. Choosing only one is typically the hardest part. Whether I'm in the mood for an appetizer or salad, pasta or rice dish, chicken or beef or vegetarian, or a dessert to finish out the night, the restaurant has it all. I pick my favorite for that day, and then I get excited to go back and on my next visit try my second favorite (that I enviously watched my friend enjoy on our previous visit). That is a good restaurant.

Let's apply this menu analogy to activity planning. In years past, I bet that you had a fuller activity menu. Maybe it was fuller when you were working and spent time with your coworkers, or before you had to move to a new area, or before finances became tight, or before you hurt your knee, or before your kids were born and shifted your activities to being kid-centric. However, when these stressors occurred, activity menu options were crossed out. For example, maybe you had to give up basketball after you hurt your knee or aged out of the local leagues.

Can you think of any reasons why your activity menu thinned out? Why did you give up on each of your previously enjoyed activities?

_____

_____

_____

Whether you can identify the reasons or not, your abandonment of activities is not the primary concern. Rather, the problem is the removal of activities *without replacing them* with alternative options. Think back to the restaurant menu. Can you imagine your favorite restaurant removing all the chicken dishes (due to a supply shortage) and not replacing them? If that pattern continued, the full menu would go down from thirty options to twenty to ten to only a handful. That surely doesn't sound very appealing. At the same time, that pattern may sound familiar. With high stress and negative emotions (and avoidance), your activity menu can take a beating. And the most complicated and fulfilling activities tend to be the first to go. Eventually, you are left with the simple (generally isolated) activities, such as watching television, taking a nap, or just "relaxing." Now, maybe when life was really busy in years past, treating yourself to a few hours of television or a midday nap was a very special and rewarding activity. However, now if that's the only thing that you're doing, it doesn't provide the same positive feelings. Doing the same couple of activities every day would be just like eating the same food daily. While I do love eating chicken wings, I cannot imagine that I would enjoy them for very long if I had to eat them daily (nor would I enjoy the results at my next physical).

It's time to change that pattern. You need to rebuild your menu. And—remembering that good restaurant menu—you need lots of choices. You need activities to do daytime and nighttime, on hot days and cold days, on rainy days and sunny days, inside the house and outside in the community or in nature, by yourself and with friends, on a weekday and weekend, and so on.

Identifying Positive Activities

Please check any activity that you currently enjoy, previously enjoyed, always wanted to try, considered once or twice, heard might be fun, or could try just for kicks.

- ☐ Going to the beach/river
- ☐ Going on a picnic
- ☐ Going out to dinner
- ☐ Going to a sporting event

- ☐ Camping
- ☐ Going to a local event
- ☐ Window shopping
- ☐ Going to the library/bookstore

- ☐ Visiting an old friend
- ☐ Calling a friend
- ☐ Road trip
- ☐ Going to a museum/park

- ☐ Visiting family
- ☐ Calling family
- ☐ Going to a movie
- ☐ Swimming

- ☐ Biking
- ☐ Fishing
- ☐ Walking/jogging
- ☐ Golf

- ☐ Playing card games
- ☐ Board games
- ☐ Nature watching
- ☐ Completing puzzles

- ☐ Boating
- ☐ Pool/billiards
- ☐ Reading
- ☐ Writing stories/poetry/blog

- ☐ Taking a class
- ☐ Cleaning house
- ☐ Hiking
- ☐ Cooking something special

- ☐ Yard work
- ☐ Gardening
- ☐ Art/crafts
- ☐ Rearranging a room

- ☐ Fixing things
- ☐ Working on a car
- ☐ Playing an instrument
- ☐ Singing/dancing

- ☐ Photography
- ☐ Woodworking
- ☐ Buying something
- ☐ Going to gym

- ☐ Playing with a pet
- ☐ Meditation/yoga
- ☐ Listening to music
- ☐ Volunteer work

- ☐ Doing favors for others
- ☐ Going to church
- ☐ Joining a local group
- ☐ Hunting

- ☐ Other Social: _____
- ☐ Other Accomplishment: _____
- ☐ Other Physical: _____
- ☐ Other Skill: _____
- ☐ Other: _____
- ☐ Other: _____

Now that you have some options, let's return to Patricia's example to see how positive emotional exposures can be applied to stop avoiding and start living.

Patricia's Story (continued)

When Patricia arrived to treatment, her positive emotional avoidance had led her to reduced positive emotions and growing negative emotions over time. She had become isolated and alone, despite living around the corner from family members and lifelong friends. Her mother had confronted Patricia and convinced her that it was time for change, which led her to my office.

We started by creating a new menu for her and selecting new activities to complete each week. Although her new activities appeared interesting, and she scheduled them at convenient times, Patricia initially struggled to engage in the activities. She blamed her lack of motivation and energy on her lack of exposure progress, which is a common complaint when dealing with positive emotional avoidance. In fact, lack of interest, motivation, energy, and drive are all common symptoms of depression and positive emotional avoidance by definition. She was not engaging in activities because she was depressed, and that very same set of depressive symptoms robbed her of the ability to push herself to engage in new activities. It took Patricia tremendous effort, forcing herself into these activities, to cause the change to happen. Just like forcing yourself to face your negative emotions in situational exposures, Patricia had to force herself to do her activities regardless of her depression, to fight through her avoidance and feel better. The initial couple of activities were slow at first. She forced herself to spend time with her nieces and nephews (because she had always enjoyed time with kids in the past) and then added a coffee date with one of her coworkers. With each activity, she started to feel a little better, and the activities felt less forced and more normal. Patricia added new activities, such as picking up jewelry making (after buying a random kit during a forced window-shopping trip) and daily walks through area parks (purposely stopping to smell the flowers). Over time, Patricia had a new and fuller menu, and she found her way to feeling well again.

Now it's your turn to incorporate positive emotional exposures into your weekly schedule and start rebuilding your activity menu. Please keep in mind that these exposures differ only in the initial emotions experienced (numbing or disinterest rather than strong negative emotions). Otherwise, they should work much the same. The key to success with positive emotional exposures is in the diversity and frequency of choices (you don't know what's enjoyable to you, or you'd already be doing it, so you have to try a lot of things) and in the scheduling of the activities (you're really going to need to force yourself into these activities so pick specific days and times to do them). And so, in terms of positive emotional exposures, it probably is the best homework assignment that you've ever had. It's time to focus on enjoying yourself again.

For now, please reference your expanded Record of Avoidance, treatment goals, and Exposure Rules to assign new exposures for the week in the tracker that follows. Also, take a look at your progress from last week's exposures in the categories listed earlier in this chapter. Use it as a guide to where to increase the difficulty and repeat for additional learning. Revisiting our original examples in week 4, schedule a lot of exposures and schedule them on specific days and times to improve your chances at continued success on your journey to stop avoiding and start living.

Exposure Tracking Worksheet

	Planned Exposure	Scheduled Day/Time	Initial Symptoms (–100 to +100)	Peak Symptoms (–100 to +100)	Final Symptoms (–100 to +100)	Total Time
Examples						
Situational	Shop at grocery store	Tuesday @ 2 p.m.	–50	–80	–40	45min
Positive emotional	Attending baseball game	Saturday @ 1 p.m.	–10	+50	+40	90 min
1						
2						
3						
4						
5						
6						
7						
8						

	Planned Exposure	Scheduled Day/Time	Initial Symptoms (–100 to +100)	Peak Symptoms (–100 to +100)	Final Symptoms (–100 to +100)	Total Time
9						
10						
11						
12						
13						
14						
15						
16						
17						
18						

Now that your exposures are planned, it's that time again. Time to make sure that you don't forget what you have planned. You should have a system worked out by now. Whether it be hard copies posted throughout your house or events on your shared online calendar, please keep it going. This is not the time to let up. Be the hero of your story and continue practicing the exposures.

WRAPPING UP

After checking on your symptoms and reviewing your exposure practices, this chapter revealed a new twist in your journey to overcome avoidance. It turns out that there are four types of avoidance that you may be experiencing and leading to your increased negative emotions (and decreased positive emotions). You learned that situational, physical, and thought avoidance are associated with increased negative emotions (so you may be avoiding not just situations that cause you to feel worse, but also physical sensations and thoughts). And you learned that positive emotional avoidance is caused by your anticipated lack of positive emotions (so you may avoid situations because you think that they won't make you feel any better). We revised your standard exposure practices and rules to target these four types of avoidance. Although the revised exposures vary little from the exposures that you have been using for weeks, they still have some important differences that are crucial for you to incorporate into your journey. This information will be critical in the weeks ahead.

In the next chapter, we will check in more fully on your symptom progress and exposure practices. During your upcoming practices, you'll want to be on the lookout for any obstacles that may have been interfering with your exposure success. We will be labeling these. Rather than the established types of avoidance, these impediments may be getting in the way of trying your planned exposures, and you will learn how to handle them, too. No matter the obstacle, you will work through it. Nothing can stop you now.

Step Further into the Life You Want

You have six chapters completed at this point. I expect that exposures have become a powerful and effective tool for you in your fight against avoidance, and that defeating avoidance has indeed resulted in positive changes in how you feel, both reducing the times that you feel badly and increasing times of pleasant feelings. In this chapter, we are going to hit pause and see how far you have come on your journey. You will do your standard symptom check-in and tracking, and then carefully inspect your answers to each of the questions. We will use those specific answers to direct your future selections of exposures. You also will start the search for any obstacles standing in your path to exposure success. We will label these obstacles as strategies that avoidance is using to keep you busy and away from challenging it directly. Our goal in this chapter is to put the final touches on your exposures as you advance toward the finish line in your journey to stop avoiding and start living.

SEARCHING FOR LINGERING DARK CLOUDS

It's time to complete your weekly assessment with the Symptom Checklist. You likely have gotten very used to these items over the weeks. In fact, you may be just skimming them at this point. That is expected with any repeat behavior. However, I want you to go through these items *with greater attention to detail* than in previous weeks. Please read each item fully and carefully. Your specific answers to the specific questions will be used to further tailor your treatment. Ready? Please complete and tally your score and enter it and today's date in the Symptom Tracking Form. This will be your sixth score. Your pattern of symptom improvements should be headed in the right direction. We just need to make sure that we aren't leaving anything behind.

Symptom Checklist	Not at all	A little	Moderately	Very much so
1. Depressed mood, most of the day, nearly every day	0	1	2	3
2. Avoidance of people, places, and situations (e.g., crowds)	0	1	2	3
3. Feeling constantly on guard and preparing for danger (e.g., back to the wall)	0	1	2	3
4. Frequent periods of intense anxiety or panic	0	1	2	3
5. Avoidance of physical sensations (e.g., heart racing, heavy breathing)	0	1	2	3
6. Avoidance of unpleasant thoughts or memories (e.g., of a car accident)	0	1	2	3
7. Loss of interest or pleasure, most of the day, nearly every day	0	1	2	3
8. Avoidance of activities that were previously enjoyed (e.g., working out)	0	1	2	3
Total Score:				
Date:				

Now that you have completed the questionnaire, it is time to look for areas of greater need. Although you likely have been engaged in a series of different exposure practices over the preceding weeks, all exposures are not equally doable or effective. It is likely that some symptoms are still causing you difficulty, while others have improved more rapidly. Please review your checklist answers to match any elevated scores in the item groups that follow. It's a concern if you either score any 3s or 4s on your questionnaire items or score higher on a single item or two compared to the rest of the items (scoring a 2 on one item when the rest of the items are 0 or 1). By searching for any dark clouds where avoidance and isolation may be lingering, you will be able to further tailor more impactful exposure practices that will greatly affect how close you are to your treatment goals.

Storm Cloud #1: Elevated scores for items 1, 7, or 8 (depressed mood, loss of interest, avoidance of previously enjoyed activities).

Higher scoring for one or more of these items suggest that you are continuing to experience difficulties with symptoms of depression and positive emotional avoidance. These symptoms may involve feeling particularly down or sad, unable to feel up, motivated, or energized, or both. Either way, the primary treatment approach for these symptoms is *positive emotional exposures*. Please return to the Identifying Positive Activities worksheet in week 6 and select more activities to try; add these to your Exposure Tracking Form at the end of the chapter. The key for these exposures is to have as many menu options as possible. However, symptoms of depression (lack of interest, motivation, and drive) are by their very nature likely to make most of your menu options appear uninteresting. Accordingly, I expect that it's been a while since you've engaged in most of these activities. And that is the point of these practices. You haven't been engaging in pleasant activities, so you haven't been feeling pleasant. You'll need to *force yourself* to try as many of these activities as possible.

If you continue to struggle to find activities, another option may be to shop for activities. With this approach, you need to go to places where pleasant activities may be found. You could go to the library and force yourself to browse for an hour for both books to read (novels, nonfiction, or graphic novels) and look for activities at the same time by searching the stacks on hobbies, such as gardening, cooking, or camping. You also could go to the hobby store and force yourself to browse for an hour to find a model to build, card game to learn, board game to play, or drone to fly. Browsing the craft store is another way to identify interesting activities, such as sewing or knitting a new pattern, carving or wood burning, or scrapbooking. If you continue to struggle while shopping for activities, you could enter each of these locations with a required goal, such as not leaving until you have spent $20 or borrowed five books.

Another key to building your menu and filling in your schedule is the selection of *new activities*. You probably have a few activities that you already stay busy with, such as watching television, mowing the lawn, or cleaning the dishes (none of which are particularly enjoyable). Although you need to keep doing some of them (if you want a maintained lawn or clean dishes), if ordinary recurring chores or passive TV consumption are all you spend your time on, you should expect to continue to feel the same way (depressed). Using the menu example, it would be similar to eating the same thing every day. Just as a variety of appetizing menu options is critical to restaurant success, so too is a variety of new and interesting pleasant activity options critical to your success. And that will not happen unless you try lots and lots of new activities.

It's understandable that after years of limited positive emotions and lots of negative emotions you may not know what you enjoy anymore. It is your quest now to try as many sample activities as possible to create your own new and improved activity menu.

What social activities can you add?

_____

_____

What new hobbies can you add?

_____

_____

What new outdoor activities can you add?

_____

_____

What new indoor activities can you add?

_____

_____

What physically active activities can you add?

_____

_____

Where will you shop for new activities (be specific)?

_____

_____

Please be sure to incorporate these recommendations into your next Exposure Tracking Worksheet.

Storm Cloud #2: Elevated scores for items 2 or 3 (avoidance of situations, preparing for danger).

Elevated scores on one or more of these items suggest continued difficulties with situational avoidance. This is the type of exposure that has received the most attention thus far in the book. Assuming that you have been completing several situational exposures weekly and staying long enough to learn the outcome of each exposure, there are a few possible explanations for continued difficulties in this area. First, it is important to determine whether these symptoms have changed over time or the scores have remained elevated all of this time. More specifically, it may be that your situational avoidance has improved (decreased from 4 to 3 or from 4 or 3 to 2 from the first to the sixth assessment) but remains elevated compared to your other symptoms. If change is occurring, you are in good shape. Just keep up what you're doing, and time will take care of the rest.

If your symptoms have not improved over time, there are a couple of explanations related to your original Exposure Rules. The first possibility is related to the third rule: expect to feel uncomfortable in the situation. Your exposures need to continuously increase in difficulty. Just as with working out, you need to continue to push yourself to make gains. More specifically, if you want to be able to run a 10k race, you should not limit yourself to running one mile at a time. You'll need to steadily increase the distance until you're able to complete the six-plus miles. Exposure practices work in the same manner. If your treatment goal is to complete your own weekly grocery shopping, you cannot limit yourself to short trips to the convenience store (even if that is an improvement over previously being dependent on family members). You will need to push yourself to a grocery store. In fact, you may want to push yourself even further (a discount warehouse or big box store) to get over this avoidance.

Which activities do you need to push yourself harder to complete successfully?

_____

_____

What exposures should be added to push yourself further?

_____

_____

Another explanation is associated with the Exposure Rule #5: don't use safety behaviors during your exposures. Safety behaviors are any action that you use to lessen your experience of negative emotions when confronting avoidance. In week 4, we discussed the use of alcohol or drugs immediately before, during, or immediately after completing an exposure. We also discussed the safety behavior of going into exposures only while accompanied by an "exposure buddy." But there are a many more activities that can serve as safety behaviors that may be limiting your gains from situational exposure practices.

Identifying Safety Behaviors

Please check *any* safety behaviors that you have used in your exposures to reduce your negative emotion.

☐ Carrying medication

☐ Drinking alcohol before, during, or after

☐ Carrying weapon

☐ Keeping back to the wall

☐ Only going in empty aisles

☐ Sitting in back row

☐ Sitting at the end of the row

☐ Staying near the exits

☐ Taking mood-altering medication before, during, or after

☐ Sitting with an exit in view

☐ Only going out during the day

☐ Only driving in the slow lane

☐ Only driving on back roads

☐ Only going with a friend or family member

☐ Only going late at night

☐ Only going during off hours

☐ Avoiding eye contact

☐ Wearing bulky clothing

☐ Repeatedly checking on things

☐ Seeking reassurance

☐ Repeatedly washing your hands

☐ Counting

☐ Sticking to the corners in social gatherings

☐ Other: _____

☐ Other: _____

☐ Other: _____

Any one of these safety behaviors may be limiting your treatment gains. In future practices, please attempt to stop your use of safety behaviors. You could slowly remove them over time (plan exposures later and later in the day until you are out at night), or simply stop them completely right away (plan exposure at midnight).

How do you plan to eliminate your safety behaviors?

_____

_____

_____

Please be sure to incorporate these recommendations into your next Exposure Tracking Worksheet.

Storm Cloud #3: Elevated scores for items 4 or 5 (intense anxiety and physical avoidance).

A higher score on one or more of these items suggests continued difficulties with physical avoidance. These exposures were just introduced in week 6. Physical exposures involve repeatedly exposing yourself to physical sensations (heart racing, rapid breathing, dizziness, difficulty breathing) to break the connection between negative emotions and physical sensations, and thereby reducing physical avoidance. These practices will take time to work. It is not surprising to have continued physical avoidance after only one week of physical exposure practices. However, if you are having difficulty trying these types of exposures due to intense anxiety and fear (fear of having a heart attack or stroke), please review the description of panic attacks in week 1. Again, panic attacks and the associated physical sensations are part of the fight-or-flight system that is specifically intended to keep you alive in the face of danger. In light of that purpose, you can see why these sensations cannot and will not harm you. It also may be helpful to repeat the physical challenge activities in week 6 to determine which sensations are continuing to cause strong negative emotions and avoidance.

Which physical sensations continue to cause you strong negative emotions?

_____

_____

_____

What types of physical exposures can you use to address these sensations?

_____

_____

_____

Please be sure to incorporate these recommendations into your next Exposure Tracking Worksheet.

Storm Cloud #4: Elevated score for item 6 (thought avoidance).

Elevations on this item suggest continued difficulties with thought avoidance. Similar to the physical exposures, thought exposures were just introduced in week 6 and will take time to become effective. Thought exposures involve repeatedly exposing yourself to traumatic or highly unpleasant thoughts or memories. It is not surprising to have continued thought avoidance after only one week of thought exposure practices. However, if you are having difficulty trying these types of exposures, there are a few techniques you could use to improve your practices and related symptom improvements.

One area of improvement may be the level of detail that you include in your exposure recording or narrative writing. The exposure practice should be limited largely to the details of the event itself and the immediate aftermath. Do your best to limit the information at the start of the retelling. And although you want it to include the details in your "movie" (using present tense and multiple sensory descriptions), you do not want to get lost in the details by including too much information (or conversely, constrain your description with too little information), which could limit your emotional reaction to the exposure. As stated in the Exposure Rules in week 4, you *should* experience increased negative emotions during these exposures. If you are not (but are still experiencing thought avoidance), you'll need to adjust the level of detail of your exposure accordingly.

Another potential area of improvement is remaining present and focused during the retelling of the thought exposure. You should limit distractions during the exposures. This means finding a quiet and private area to complete your exposures. It's natural to have your mind wander during thought exposures to other unrelated topics. You can challenge this type of avoidance by shifting between audio recording and written narratives or using a physical cue to snap your mind back on to the retelling (one common method is keeping a rubber band around your wrist and snapping it periodically during the exposure).

A third area of improvement is bringing the traumatic or highly unpleasant thoughts or memories out into the open. Again, thought avoidance is associated with repeated efforts to *stop thinking* about the memory, which is more or less impossible. You cannot tell yourself to not think about a pink elephant and expect that you won't think about the pink elephant in the process. And so, the goal of thought exposures is stop hiding from the memory through repeated rehearsals. Thus far, I have presented the thought exposures as private exercises to overcome thought avoidance. However, they do not have to be private. As with the example of Earl, the sharing of your traumatic or highly unpleasant thoughts or memories with others can be a very powerful and effective approach to defeat thought avoidance.

Which traumatic or highly unpleasant thoughts or memories continue to cause you urges to avoid due to associated strong negative emotions?

_____

_____

_____

In what ways can you improve your thought exposures to further address thought avoidance?

_____

_____

_____

Please be sure to incorporate these recommendations into your next Exposure Tracking Worksheet.

REVIEWING YOUR PAST WEEK'S EXPOSURE PRACTICES

It is time to check in on your weekly scheduled exposure practices. At this point, the expectation is that most of your past exposure practices have become new routines. Now you simply go grocery shopping or go out to lunch with friends, rather than having to assign yourself those types of activities as your weekly homework. In fact, it could be you've already defeated one thing that you have been avoiding for some time. If so, that is extraordinary. I hope that you (and your friends and family) are pleased by your successes. They were well earned.

However, in my experience, it's unlikely that you have reached all of your treatment goals yet. It is that unfinished business that we need to investigate here.

How did your exposures go over the past week? Describe your overall experience, writing down the most important elements.

_____

_____

_____

How did it go tailoring your exposures to the specific kind of avoidance you have been experiencing? Were they more helpful? Harder? Or easier?

_____

_____

_____

As in previous chapters, let's look at your exposure practices. To save you the need to flip back in the book, I have listed updated possible outcomes and problem-solving for exposures that continue to present difficulties. Review your exposure tracking form and match up your practices to these categories.

Outcome #1: You tried some exposures and did not experience negative emotions.

In contrast to previous explanations (trying exposures that are not difficult enough), I expect that your response to exposures in this category is being influenced by your treatment gains. Whereas in the past these exposures may have caused urges to avoid and strong negative emotions (or lack of positive emotions), now they simply do not cause you any difficulties. If that's the case, it is time to cross that item off your expanded Record of Avoidance and check the status of your treatment goals, and move to the next item on your list (if any remain).

If it is not associated with treatment gains, other possible explanations for this experience are either picking an exposure that wasn't difficult enough or due to the use of safety behaviors. Safety behaviors are detailed earlier in this chapter. Please increase the difficulty of the exposure and lessen or remove your safety behaviors and repeat the exposure.

Outcome #2: You tried exposures and learned a little from (almost stayed long enough).

As described in week 5, this outcome may be associated with not knowing your reason for avoiding the activity. You should define your anticipated negative outcome before you embark on your exposure practice, with a way to test it out. For example, if you are afraid that you will be violently attacked if you shop at night, you should set a specific amount of time for testing whether the attack will take place. How much time or number of practices do you think you need to test out your anticipated negative outcome? Pursuing the shopping at night example, you need to determine how many times that you need to walk through a dark parking lot to prove to your satisfaction that you won't be attacked. After you have walked through it that many times, you promise yourself that you'll accept the updated outcome (no attack), once and for all, and your urges to avoid and your related negative emotions, should reduce.

Although a previous alternative explanation for this outcome suggested that you had tried exposures that were too hard, at this point I do not think that is the case. Once you have completed a good number of exposures, none of them should be "too difficult." Unlike past comparisons to lifting heavy weights or running long distances that require continuous training, monitoring, and progress, exposures simply require the willingness to try them and the time to challenge and learn about your anticipated negative outcome. The more difficult the exposure, the more knowledge there is to be gained at this point.

Outcome #5: You tried some exposures and did not learn from them (left too early) and Outcome #6: You completed some exposures, but you did not try others.

It is common to continue to have some exposures that are causing you these types of difficulties. However, unlike previous explanations involving difficulty level or time available to complete them, here I want to shift to another set of explanations. Although exposures are a powerful tool in the fight against avoidance and the resulting negative emotions, there may be associated symptoms that interfere with your ability to use your exposures effectively. Let's look at these obstacles, because they may be why you continue to have difficulty in some exposures.

IDENTIFYING YOUR OBSTACLES

Obstacles are specific symptoms that are interfering with your ability to complete your exposures as assigned. While not everyone runs into these types of challenges, they can be quite frustrating to some as they lessen (or prevent) the benefits of some exposures. These obstacles are not necessary external factors, such as available time, transportation, or friends or family. Rather, these obstacles are associated physical sensations, thoughts, or behaviors.

Can you think of any internal obstacles that have interfered with your exposure practices?

_____

_____

_____

Obstacle #1: Negative thought patterns.

Negative thought patterns can prevent practice and learning during the exposure process. These thoughts can be depressive, such as *I'll never get better*, or *I shouldn't even try*, or fearful, such as *I'm going to die if I try that* or *I'm going to explode if I get stuck in that traffic*. With these types of thoughts, exposure may not be particularly effective because they tend to lead to minimal practice. Negative thought patterns are common and generally improve with repeated exposure practices, as you test and learn from the anticipated negative outcome. However, when negative thought patterns interfere with engaging in exposure practices altogether, you may need to give additional attention to coming up with coping statements to improve your exposure practices and related outcomes.

The first step in working with negative thoughts is attempting to identify them as they are happening. This may be challenging at first, as we may not necessarily think about our thoughts. It may be helpful to think of those cartoon images in which a little angel (the good voice) and a little devil (the bad voice) perch on one's shoulders to whisper advice in your ears.

What negative thoughts have you noticed? Can you think of any negative thoughts that you tend to have before, during, or after exposures?

_____

_____

_____

Once you've identified the negative thoughts, it's time to try to fight back with coping statements. You need to find a way to knock the little devil off your shoulder, by supplying your little angel with good things to say to encourage you in your exposure practices. These statements can include any self-talk that can quickly help you to move more to the center—not overly negative but also not overly positive. Let's return to our original example of Tommy and his cat fears from week 4. If Tommy's little devil is screaming *The cat will attack me if I get too close*, that statement would likely keep Tommy from ever getting used to the cat, much less petting it (avoiding the exposure practice). However, simply thinking positively, such as *All cats are nice and friendly*, also may not accurately capture the situation (especially since in fact all cats are *not* nice and friendly). Instead, it's important to find a balance between the positive and negative thoughts, such as *While the cat might scratch me, the cat cannot seriously injury me*. The statement both finds a balance between the negative and positive thoughts as well as encourages Tommy to engage in the exposure practice.

Now that you understand the process, let's figure out how to get you there. At first, you will need to take the process a little slower as you learn how to think more about your thinking. You will need to write out the negative thoughts and possible rebuttals or coping statements for each exposure. The following worksheet can be useful in slowing down the process. It encourages you to track your thoughts in one exposure at a time.

Incorporating Coping Statements into Exposures

Planned Initial Exposure: _____

Date/Time	Initial Emotions −100 (neg) to +100 (pos)	Peak Emotions −100 (neg) to +100 (pos)	Final Emotions −100 (neg) to +100 (pos)	Total Time Engaged in Exposure

Physical Sensations What are you feeling?	Negative Thoughts What are you thinking?	Behaviors What are you doing?

Eventually, with practice, you will get increasingly better at anticipating negative thoughts and planning with specific coping statements prior to embarking on your exposures. Put more simply, you will welcome back the angel on your shoulder and give that little helper the needed statements to overcome the arguments of the devil on your other shoulder and reclaim your exposure practices. And in the end, you will send the devil packing as you stop avoiding and starting living.

You may find the following adapted Exposure Tracking Worksheet useful when incorporating coping statements into your exposures. This slightly different worksheet includes one new column for planning your coping statement(s) for your exposure practices beforehand. You may want to start with the Incorporating Coping Statements into Exposures Worksheet until you have had success with coping statements, then shift to using the adapted Exposure Tracking Worksheet. Additional copies can be printed from http://www.newharbinger.com/45663.

Exposure Tracking Worksheet (with Coping Statements)

	Planned Exposure	Scheduled Day/Time	Planned Coping Statement	Initial Symptoms (–100 to +100)	Peak Symptoms (–100 to +100)	Final Symptoms (–100 to +100)	Total Time
Examples							
Situational	Shop at grocery store	Tuesday @ 2 p.m.	They are just symptoms. They cannot hurt me.	–50	–80	–40	45min
1							
2							
3							
4							
5							
6							
7							
8							

Planned Exposure	Scheduled Day/Time	Planned Coping Statement	Initial Symptoms (–100 to +100)	Peak Symptoms (–100 to +100)	Final Symptoms (–100 to +100)	Total Time
9						
10						
11						
12						
13						
14						
15						
16						
17						
18						

Obstacle #2: Sleep disruption.

Disrupted sleep can reduce your energy, motivation, and drive. In fact, the symptoms of poor sleep can mimic those associated with depression. And poor sleep can give you an irresistible urge to stay in bed longer in the morning, difficulty leaving the couch, and lengthy naps during the day. Inactivity and naps during the day can be associated with difficulty sleeping at night, further worsening the problems on the following day. All of these behaviors are associated with fewer exposure practices and thus fewer treatment gains. Although positive emotional exposures will be helpful (filling up the daytime with positive activities), you may find that you need separate sleep-specific practices to improve your exposure success.

This section is meant to focus on sleep disruption when it interferes with exposure, but honestly, nearly everyone could benefit from getting better sleep, independent of their negative emotions and related exposure successes. Let's start with a few questions about your sleep.

What type of sleep problems are you having? Check all that apply.

☐ 1.   Difficulty falling asleep

☐ 2.   Frequent wake-ups in the middle of the night

☐ 3.   Lengthy wake-ups in the middle of the night

☐ 4.   Difficulty getting out of bed in the morning

☐ 5.   Intense fatigue during the day

☐ 6.   Daytime napping

☐ 7.   Not sleeping enough (less than seven hours daily)

☐ 8.   Sleeping too much (more than nine hours daily)

☐ 9.   Checking the doors, windows, and yard during the night

☐ 10. Being woken up by the slightest noises at night

Okay, now that we've identified the types of sleep disruption that you are experiencing, it is time to match them to a new treatment technique for improving your sleep and energy level, which in turn can improve your exposure practices. In particular, we will focus on improving your sleep-related behaviors to relieve your fatigue, because fatigue can negatively influence your exposure practices. The goal is that with the successful incorporation of these new techniques your energy level will improve, allowing for improved exposure practices as well.

The primary reason for focusing on these symptoms and related behaviors is that they may prevent practice and learning during the exposure process. Let's return to the case of Tommy and his fear of cats in week 4. We originally outlined a set of possible exposures to help Tommy overcome his negative emotions, such as repeatedly going over his friends home to be around the cat. However, let's give Tommy some sleep problems and related fatigue. Let's say that Tommy ends up skipping numerous exposures to the cat, because he's too tired, needs a midday nap, or has general lack of motivation due to his fatigue. Alternatively, Tommy may begin the exposure but become distracted by fatigue during the practice and ultimately cut it short.

This example may be less common in situational exposure. A more apt example may be falling asleep in a movie theater during a positive emotional exposure and not enjoying the movie as a result. In both examples, the exposure is not likely to be particularly effective.

Here is a list of new rules for your sleep behaviors, what we call *sleep hygiene*. Just as how a dentist encourages better dental hygiene following a cavity or a doctor encourages better hand hygiene following a cold, we need to encourage better sleep hygiene to improve your sleep, daytime fatigue, and related exposure practices. Please review the following list; the numbers from the preceding sleep assessment are matched to the corresponding item to show where you should focus your attention.

Rules to Improve Your Sleep (check any that apply):

☐ 1.   Set the alarm for a planned, consistent wake-up time every day of (insert time): _____. You cannot sleep a minute longer than the set alarm time. Get out of bed immediately (no snooze button).

Helpful for items 1, 2, 3, 4, 5, 6, 7, 8

☐ 2.   No naps at all. No matter what. Sleep is allowed *only* between a set bedtime and set wake time. This also goes for "resting your eyes" or spending long periods of time half-asleep and inactive, such as lying on the couch watching a lot of television.

Helpful for items 1, 2, 3, 6, 7, 8

☐ 3.   No caffeine after lunch. No eating or drinking one hour before bedtime.

Helpful for items 1, 2, 3, 7, 10

☐ 4.   Before bedtime, set up a quiet time in preparation for bedtime at (insert time): _____ with planned activities of (insert boring activities that lack screen time) : _____. Quiet time should not take place in bed. Activities should be not particularly active, such as reading a boring book or emptying the dishwasher. Do not engage in activities that can cause negative emotions, such as checking locks or looking out windows.

Helpful for items 1, 5, 6, 9

☐ 5.   Go to bed only when you are tired, but try to make it a planned, consistent bedtime every night, around (insert time): _____. Do not go to bed too early due to fatigue. Push yourself to wait at least until your scheduled time.

Helpful for items 1, 2, 3, 5, 6, 7, 8, 10

☐ 6.   Turn off lights and all electronics (absolutely no TV in bed), put away reading materials, and turn on a noise generator (phone application or white noise on the radio).

Helpful for items 1, 2, 3, 4, 7, 10

☐ 7.   Do not stay in bed awake for more than twenty minutes. If you can't sleep, return to quiet time (step 4) until you get tired again. Do not engage in any checking behaviors (no checking the locks or looking out the windows). Then return to bed and give yourself another twenty minutes. Repeat the process as needed to retrain your body to know to sleep while in bed (rather than to lie awake for hours).

Helpful for items 2, 3, 4, 5, 6, 9

Please make a real effort to add these new behaviors and rules into your daily sleep routine. They tend to be quite helpful in improving nighttime sleep and reducing daytime fatigue when used regularly. It is important to note that there is no perfect way to sleep. Each of us has slightly different needs. You may or may not be able to sleep with a noise generator; however, you absolutely should not be trying to sleep with a TV on in the bedroom. That said, you may not have to incorporate all of these new rules from the start. You can try layering them in one at a time to see which are most helpful. However, regardless of your approach, it is critical to improve your sleep and daytime fatigue to help you stop avoiding and start living.

Given the potential influence of disrupted sleep and daytime fatigue, I have included a customized Exposure Tracking Worksheet to help you to track your sleep and fatigue and their influence on your exposure practices. Additional copies can be printed from http://www.newhar

binger.com/45663. If you find that your exposures are not going as well on days with poor sleep and heightened fatigue, you should work to incorporate more of these new sleep rules into your daily routine.

Exposure Tracking Worksheet (with Sleep Tracking)

	Planned Exposure	Scheduled Day/ Time	Total Sleep Last Night	Fatigue Severity (−100 to 0)	Initial Symptoms (−100 to +100)	Peak Symptoms (−100 to +100)	Final Symptoms (−100 to +100)	Total Time
Examples								
Situational	Shop at grocery store	Tuesday @ 2 p.m.	4 hours	−60	−50	−80	−40	45min
1								
2								
3								
4								
5								
6								
7								
8								

	Planned Exposure	Scheduled Day/ Time	Total Sleep Last Night	Fatigue Severity (-100 to 0)	Initial Symptoms (−100 to +100)	Peak Symptoms (−100 to +100)	Final Symptoms (−100 to +100)	Total Time
9								
10								
11								
12								
13								
14								
15								
16								
17								
18								

Obstacle #3: Alcohol or drug use.

Although alcohol and drug use was identified as a potential safety behavior in previous sections, it also can be a stand-alone problem associated with fewer exposure practices and related poorer outcomes. In fact, alcohol and drug use also can be characterized as another type of avoidance, in that it contributes to the development of more negative emotions. You may need additional assessment and practices to assist with better managing your alcohol and drug use to improve your exposure practices.

For example, if you are consuming fifteen drinks or more per week, using street drugs (cocaine, heroin, methamphetamine), or abusing prescription medications (pain medications, sedatives, stimulants) and fear that this may be causing significant problems in your life (at work, with the law, in your relationships), you may be experiencing concerning alcohol or drug use that requires specialized treatment. Although that type of use is outside the scope of this section, the Substance Abuse and Mental Health Services Administration (SAMHSA) and similar programs have made it easy to find local services that can help you. You can start the process by calling the SAMHSA National Helpline at 1-800-662-HELP (1-800-662-4357). This 24/7, 365-days-a-year hotline serves as a free and confidential treatment referral and information service within the United States. It is an excellent place to start.

In terms of this treatment, we will focus on mild alcohol or marijuana use not causing associated stand-alone problems in life (work, legal, or social). Our concern is with whether alcohol or marijuana are interfering with your negative emotions and related exposure success. In fact, alcohol and drug use are often described as "drinking to cope" with negative emotions. This section may be helpful to you if you are drinking alcohol or using marijuana (1) immediately before attempting an exposure (for example, having a few drinks before going to social outing that you typically avoid), (2) while completing an exposure (for example, having a few drinks to calm down at a crowded sporting event), or (3) immediately following an exposure practice (for example, using marijuana to relax following a stressful thought exposure to a traumatic memory). In contrast, consuming two or fewer drinks per day may not be of concern if this consumption is separate from your negative emotions and exposure practices.

The specific nature of alcohol use means our example of Tommy's cat fear does not fit particularly well here. Let's imagine instead Phillip, an adult with anxiety in and avoidance of social situations. In treatment, situational exposures are tried to address negative emotions; however,

Phillip's anxiety increases prior to his exposures and he turns to alcohol to calm down. By the time that he leaves for his social outing, Phillip tends to be a little drunk, putting himself at risk for both physical danger and legal trouble (driving under the influence) and limiting his benefits from his exposures (learning that he needs to drink to face his negative emotions). Phillip's "drinking to cope" behaviors also put him at risk for continued drinking and the risks associated with it.

Let's start by investigating your alcohol or marijuana use.

How has alcohol or marijuana interfered with your negative emotions?

_____

_____

_____

How has alcohol or marijuana interfered with your exposure practices and related learning (immediately before, during, or immediately after)?

_____

_____

_____

The first step in addressing alcohol or drug use concerns is daily monitoring. I'd like for you to track your use on the worksheet that follows for one week. Pay particular attention to the behaviors or triggers and negative emotions that may surround your use. I am most interested in determining both your overall use and any use to cope with or avoid your negative emotions. Use before, during, or immediately after exposure practices also is of particular concern. In those cases, substance use can be seen as a safety behavior or subtle avoidance as described in week 4. Alcohol and marijuana use have the potential to worsen negative emotions as well as reduce the effect of the exposure practices. Here is a tracking form for you to monitor your daily use.

Alcohol/Drug Use Tracking Worksheet

Day/Time	Trigger	Before, During, or After Exposure	Negative Emotions	Strength of Emotions (−100 to +100)	Alcohol/Drug Used	Quantity	Total Time
Monday, 4 p.m.	Planning to shop at grocery store	Before	Anxious, nervous, panicky	−80	Beer	Six-pack	3 hours

Once you have gathered information on your use frequency, quantity, and triggers as well as their influence on your negative emotions and exposure practices, you need to incorporate strategies for reducing your use into your ongoing exposures. There are several techniques to try.

Setting overall use limits: When overall use is problematic (> two drinks per day; > fourteen drinks per week), we will need to set daily limits on your use. Typically, we will want to set a limit for the number of days per week on which you can use, number of drinks per day of use, and overall number of drinks per week. When use is mild to moderate, these changes may be relatively mild. However, when a large quantity of alcohol is used, these changes may need to be more significant and implemented gradually over time. Start by setting limits that match the recommended limits ($\leq$ two drinks per day; $\leq$ fourteen drinks per week) and continue to monitor your daily use to track your progress and increase your awareness of your overall use. If you continue to struggle, you may want to consider seeking additional help, such as calling the SAMSHA hotline.

Setting use timing and exposure location limits: When you are using immediately before, during, and after your exposure practices, we need to place greater focus on the timing of your use and set limits. We'll do this in two steps. First, you will need to monitor your overall drinking and set timing limits: not using for one hour before your exposures, during your exposures, or one hour after your exposures. Second, you will need to adjust your exposure practices to situations for which you can effectively manage use. For example, if exposures to crowds are generally difficult for you and trigger an urge to drink, you should limit your exposures to crowds to those situations in which alcohol is less available (family movie theater), rather than situations where alcohol is very available (bowling alley). Although it is not like me to recommend avoidance, this is a temporary approach to improve your exposure practices in safer settings (without use triggers) to improve your negative emotions and urges to use. Over time, as you have greater control over your use and related negative emotions, the exposures with potential triggers can be reincorporated, with less risk for problematic use.

To accomplish and monitor these changes, there are two new columns added to your Exposure Tracking Worksheet to better identify and plan for potential triggers. Additional copies can be printed from http://www.newharbinger.com/45663.

Exposure Tracking Worksheet (with Substance Use Component)

Planned Exposure	Scheduled Day/ Time	Possible Trigger	Coping Strategy	Initial Symptoms (–100 to +100)	Peak Symptoms (–100 to +100)	Final Symptoms (–100 to +100)	Total Time
Examples							
Situational Shop at grocery store	Tuesday @ 2 p.m.	Beer aisle	Skip that section	–50	–80	–40	45min
1							
2							
3							
4							
5							
6							
7							
8							

Planned Exposure	Scheduled Day/ Time	Possible Trigger	Coping Strategy	Initial Symptoms (–100 to +100)	Peak Symptoms (–100 to +100)	Final Symptoms (–100 to +100)	Total Time
9							
10							
11							
12							
13							
14							
15							
16							
17							
18							

Obstacle #4: Chronic pain.

If you suffer from chronic pain, it should be factored into your treatment. Chronic pain can be disabling for anyone, across all activities, and especially difficult activities such as exposure practices. Chronic pain can reduce your mobility and energy level and increase overall frustration; in fact, it can cause many negative emotions (depression and anger). Although positive emotional exposures can be useful (focusing on positive activities throughout the day to distract from pain and encourage improved mobility), you may need to add pain-specific practices to overcome pain-related avoidance and improve your engagement in exposure practices. Chronic pain also can make it harder for you to do your exposure practices, so you end up completing fewer of your planned exposures. No matter what specific kind of chronic pain you have, it puts you at risk of increased difficulties with your negative emotions and avoidance.

Unfortunately, due to the nature of chronic pain, our example of Tommy's cat fear doesn't fit particularly well here. Let's imagine, instead, Lisa, an adult with chronic pain who really likes dogs. However, as her chronic back and knee pain has increased, Lisa is spending less time with her dog. The long walks, running around, and playing games of fetch that they used to enjoy together now aggravate her chronic pain. And as she has cut back on their walks and play time with her dog (which were her main physical activities), Lisa's overall exercise is greatly reduced and her stiffness and pain increase. Over time, her growing pain and reduced activity lead her into depression, which requires treatment. In treatment, her therapist wants her to try positive emotional exposures to improve her positive emotions and lessen her negative emotions; however, Lisa will not participate in any positive activities that could include physical components—and she declines to participate in nonphysical activities because they aren't as interesting as her previously enjoyed physical activities. In addition, when she finally decides to attempt physical activities, Lisa pushes herself too hard, taking her dog on a long beach walk, which sets off increased knee pain that lingers for two days afterward.

Given that example, answer the following questions about your chronic pain and physical limitations.

In which areas do you experience chronic pain?

_____

_____

How is chronic pain affecting your negative emotions and avoidance?

_____

_____

_____

How has chronic pain influenced your exposure success?

_____

_____

_____

Similar to other treatment components that you've used, the first step is to increase your awareness of the physical reactions, thoughts, and behaviors associated with your pain. I'd like you to record these symptoms any time you notice that you are experiencing a pain related to your activities or to your inactivity. The pain-related behaviors and avoidance are of greatest significance.

Self-Monitoring Worksheet: Three Components of Pain

Situation (Date/Time/Duration)	Emotions –100 (high) to 0 (low)	Physical Sensations What are you feeling?	Negative Thoughts What are you thinking?	Behaviors What are you doing?
Attempted to prepare the garden for planting season for 2 hours.	Pain –70 Depression –60 Frustration –80	Shooting pain in lower back Ache in knees Soreness in arms	I shouldn't have even tried. I'm going to hurt for a week.	Pulling weeds and using tiller Stopped due to pain Lying on the couch

As was the case in the example of Lisa, pain-related avoidance can greatly interfere with the effectiveness of exposure practices. It typically presents as avoidance of any situation that may present a risk of physical pain. Common reactions are to either (1) avoid activities that you used to enjoy but cause pain now—activities such as taking your dog on a long walk—or (2) engage in the activity without pacing yourself, causing days of avoidance during the recuperation period. In both cases, pain-related avoidance was responsible for reducing engagement in positive activities. The same could be true of situational or other types of exposures that include physical activity, such as walking through a crowded store. To further improve the treatment gains you've made with exposures, you'll need to incorporate a pain management component into your treatment. More specifically, we will identify activities or situations that you are avoiding due to your pain and then specifically craft exposures to address that pain-related avoidance.

Let's turn back to our example of Lisa, who had begun to avoid walking her dog due to chronic back and knee pain. At first, Lisa was resistant to walking the dog because she could not do what she used to do without chronic pain. To accommodate her limitations and enable her to keep engaging in healthy exercise and exposure, several alterations were incorporated. First, Lisa was encouraged to pace herself to determine what distance and time was possible for her without causing significant or lasting pain. Although her previous long walks lasted up to an hour, she was encouraged to start at five minutes and slowly work up to longer durations while monitoring pain. After several trials, Lisa learned that she could complete a twenty-minute walk with her dog with a tolerable amount of pain and without any lasting effects. Second, we used brainstorming to identify alternative ways for Lisa to play with the dog with less risk of pain. For example, Lisa started using a ball throwing gun to play fetch, rather than risk hurting herself by trying to throw the ball a long distance. With these altered approaches, Lisa was able to walk her dog, play fetch, and generally enjoy time with her dog again, but with less risk and disability from her chronic pain.

We will be using a slightly different worksheet for future exposures; it includes two new columns to identify how risk of pain is related to the exposure (if applicable) and what coping strategies you plan to use to address pain-related avoidance. Review the example in the worksheet and start scheduling your new exposures with managing your pain in mind. Additional copies can be printed from http://www.newharbinger.com/45663.

Exposure Tracking Worksheet (with Pain Component)

	Planned Exposure	Scheduled Day/Time	Pain Component	Coping Strategy	Initial Symptoms (–100 to +100)	Peak Symptoms (–100 to +100)	Final Symptoms (–100 to +100)	Total Time
Example								
Situational	Shop at grocery store	Tuesday @ 2 p.m.	60 min walks cause knee pain	Pace with 30 min walks	–50	–80	–40	30 min
1								
2								
3								
4								
5								
6								
7								
8								

Planned Exposure	Scheduled Day/Time	Pain Component	Coping Strategy	Initial Symptoms (–100 to +100)	Peak Symptoms (–100 to +100)	Final Symptoms (–100 to +100)	Total Time
9							
10							
11							
12							
13							
14							
15							
16							
17							
18							

Together, these obstacles may be compounding the negative influence of your avoidance on your emotions. The first step involves being on the lookout, especially in terms of your less-successful exposures. To clarify, these obstacles are concerning only if they are interfering with your exposures and success. It is common to have sleep difficulties and chronic pain; however, it is concerning when those symptoms become obstacles to successful exposure practices. Keep an eye out for these obstacles in this week's plans (Exposure Tracking Worksheet) to determine if you'll need additional strategies to get you where you know you can go.

PLANNING NEXT WEEK'S EXPOSURES

Okay, it is that time again. In this chapter, we have focused largely on problem solving. Between your answers on the questionnaire and the successes in your exposure practices, you should have listed a number of new approaches in the previous sections. Please take those suggestions and incorporate them into this week's exposures. As with previous chapters, refer back to your expanded Record of Avoidance Worksheet and your remaining treatment goals to assign new exposures for the week. Each of these documents should provide invaluable information to aid your exposures and chase all four types of avoidance out of your life.

To schedule your exposures, use either the following Exposure Tracking Worksheet or one of the worksheets adapted to address a specific obstacle, introduced earlier in the chapter. Additional copies can be printed from http://www.newharbinger.com/45663.

Exposure Tracking Worksheet

	Planned Exposure	Scheduled Day/Time	Initial Severity (−100 to +100)	Peak Severity (−100 to +100)	Final Severity (−100 to +100)	Total Time	Obstacle Found
Examples							
Situational	Shop at grocery store	Tuesday @ 2 p.m.	50	80	40	45min	None
Positive Emotional	Workout at Gym	Wednesday @ 8 a.m.	n/a	n/a	n/a	0 min	Sleep stayed in bed
1							
2							
3							
4							
5							
6							
7							
8							

Planned Exposure	Scheduled Day/Time	Initial Severity (–100 to +100)	Peak Severity (–100 to +100)	Final Severity (–100 to +100)	Total Time	Obstacle Found
9						
10						
11						
12						
13						
14						
15						
16						
17						
18						

Now that your exposures are planned, it's time again to lock in your schedule by using the same strategies that have worked in the past. Program these in your phone, plaster your rooms in reminders, and send out text messages to the persons involved in your plans. Avoidance has not given up, and it may be benefiting from certain obstacles that are preventing your full engagement in exposures. Keep your eye out for any exposures that were less successful due to those obstacles, and use the adapted strategies to address them. Either way, though, do continue your journey as you approach your final week.

WRAPPING UP

We continued with the same pattern of checking on your symptoms and reviewing your exposure practices. However in this chapter, we dove a little deeper in terms of investigating which specific symptoms have remained elevated. Whether it be low mood and positive emotional avoidance or high anxiety and physical avoidance, it is important to further focus your exposures in the areas of most need. In addition, we reviewed your exposure practices from the previous week, with some revised categories. We introduced exposure obstacles: these can be physical sensations (chronic pain), thoughts (negative thought patterns), and behaviors (alcohol and substance use, sleep disruption). While these revisions are focused on problem solving and improving your exposure practice, some of the practices may be helpful independent of your exposure practice. For example, the improved sleep strategies may be helpful for anyone who experiences difficulties in their daily sleep habits. Please consider incorporating them; they will help.

The next chapter is the final step in your treatment journey. We will be reviewing your progress and comparing it to your original goals and the typical responses that we generally see with this type of treatment. We will introduce relapse prevention strategies to help you to maintain your treatment gains and keep your negative emotions from returning. We also will be discussing additional steps to take if there are any lingering symptoms that have remained after completing this treatment. With luck (and a lot of hard work), the end of your treatment journey will mean that you have stopped avoiding and started living again. If that's the case, it has become an enjoyable road again.

Continue Your Involvement with Relapse-Prevention Skills

Welcome to the final week. Since the last chapter, you have been honing your exposure skills and responding with increased awareness and potential adaptations to all four of the different kinds of avoidance. By practicing through this final week, you should be, by now, an exposure expert. In this chapter, we will use the occasion of our last week to do one final check-in and then spend the rest of the time discussing your progress and the goals we set at the beginning of the book. No journey in life, or in movies, is straightforward, so be ready to approach your progress with honest reflection. If there were stumbling blocks or lapses back into the avoidance, that is okay; I have a few skills for just such lapses.

FINAL SYMPTOM ASSESSMENT

It is time to complete your weekly assessment again. Please complete and score the Symptom Checklist and enter your score and today's date in the Appendix 1 Symptom Tracking Form. This will be your sixth and final score. I hope you will see a nice progression of your scores from week to week or month to month or from the beginning of treatment to the end.

Symptom Checklist	Not at all	A little	Moderately	Very much so
1. Depressed mood, most of the day, nearly every day	0	1	2	3
2. Avoidance of people, places, and situations (e.g., crowds)	0	1	2	3
3. Feeling constantly on guard and preparing for danger (e.g., back to the wall)	0	1	2	3
4. Frequent periods of intense anxiety or panic	0	1	2	3
5. Avoidance of physical sensations (e.g., heart racing, heavy breathing)	0	1	2	3
6. Avoidance of unpleasant thoughts or memories (e.g., of a car accident)	0	1	2	3
7. Loss of interest or pleasure, most of the day, nearly every day	0	1	2	3
8. Avoidance of activities that were previously enjoyed (e.g., working out)	0	1	2	3
Total Score:				
Date:				

PLOTTING YOUR PROGRESS

Now that you have all of your scores complete, it is time to plot your treatment progress to gain a visual perspective. Please copy your scores from the Appendix 1 Symptom Tracking Form into the following graph. On the Symptom Progression graph in figure 8.1, your symptom severity appears on the y-axis (vertical) and your assessment points over time on the x-axis (left to right). Enter each of your scores in the corresponding data points, then connect the dots to create a line graph. Additional copies of the form can be printed from http://www.newharbinger.com/45663.

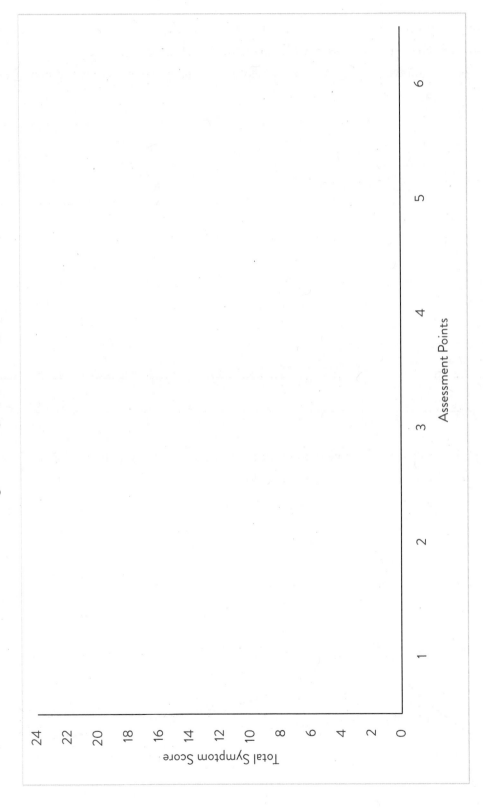

Figure 8.1. Symptom Progression

You likely have been aware of the progression both in terms of glancing at the Symptom Checklist in each chapter as well as how you have been feeling as you have worked your way through the book. However, I find it to be very helpful to actually see the scores and how they've changed.

Looking at your progress graph, how did your symptom scores change during the course of treatment?

_____

_____

Did your changes in symptom scores meet your expectations going into treatment? If so or if not, how so?

_____

_____

_____

Although I cannot see your scores myself, I can predict one common question that you may be asking yourself at the end of treatment: why didn't my scores go to zero? When answering that question, we should discuss what is the *expected* symptom response in this type of treatment approach. Let's start by looking at figure 8.2.

Figure 8.2. Three Phases of Treatment

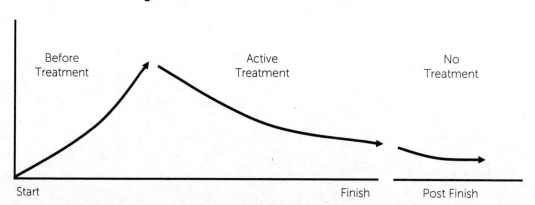

The figure depicts three phases of treatment. The first phase tracks the severity of your symptoms prior to beginning treatment. They steadily rise over time and ultimately lead you to seek help—as you remember from week 1, this is how you felt before you started the book. The second phase is the active treatment phase—the week-by-week journey that we have been on throughout this book. Hopefully, the pattern of symptoms in this stage resembles your graph from earlier in the chapter. You start off with elevated symptoms and they steadily decreased as you engaged in treatment and reached your treatment goals. However, note the end point of the active treatment phase. Although the scores during this phase start quite elevated, they *do not* finish at zero (lowest point on the y-axis).

Why do you think that treatment would stop before your symptom scores reach zero?

_____

_____

_____

The answer boils down to timing. While some people are able to reach zero quickly, most people make significant improvements during the treatment phase and then continue to make changes for the months and years afterward. The idea is that you learned the necessary skills to improve your symptoms in treatment. With the regular practice of these skills from one chapter to the next, you sought (and hopefully achieved) your treatment goals. And during that process, you started living again without avoidance. It is that stage or change that is the most important part of the treatment, and the part that will keep the symptoms away for the long term. You learned these skills, and you will not forget them. As long as you continue to practice them (or simply continue to live again without avoidance), you will continue to improve more and more over time, as depicted in the No Treatment phase.

There's another way to look at your progress. Let's compare treatment to taking a class in school, such as automotive repair. You begin the course with little knowledge (high symptoms). You sit in the class and learn new skills each week (read each chapter). You also have hands-on experiences in which you work on the car itself (completing between-chapter practices—exposures). With each class and experience, you get better at automotive repair and more confident about future procedures (symptom reduction and increasing exposure successes). When the class ends, you may not be a master mechanic, but you have the necessary skills to complete basic repairs on your car as well as how to try and learn additional repairs on your own (significant symptom gains, with ability to continue exposures on your own). And as long as you continue to complete regular maintenance on your car (live without avoidance), you will never forget those skills and will continue to get better and better at them over time (achieving continued symptom reduction).

Now you have completed your own class on negative emotions. You have learned about negative emotions and the primary mechanism that was contributing to their development and their negative impact on your life (avoidance). You will be able to keep the progress going as you continue to stop avoiding, choosing instead to live the life that you want without avoidance.

FINAL CHECK-IN ON YOUR GOALS

Symptom change is absolutely essential when it comes to determining the success of treatment. However, I will argue that treatment goal achievement is even more important. From the start of treatment, we focused on your observable behaviors. These are the actions (or inactions) that were proof that negative emotions, and consequently avoidance, were causing significant difficulties in your life. Please take time now to return to week 2 and review each of your treatment goals. Each goal contained a general target as well as a specific observable and measurable change. You may recall the video camera example that we used to identify those needed areas of change. Well, let's return to a slightly revised version of that question.

If someone followed you around with a video camera, how would they know that you *no longer* have difficulties with depression, anxiety, or stress? What would they see to show how you've *overcome* your difficulties with depression, anxiety, or stress?

_____

_____

_____

More specifically, let's review how you did on each of your treatment goals. Circle your answer for each.

Treatment Goal #1:

Significantly worse   Slightly worse   No change   Slightly better   Significantly better

Treatment Goal #2:

Significantly worse   Slightly worse   No change   Slightly better   Significantly better

Treatment Goal #3:

Significantly worse   Slightly worse   No change   Slightly better   Significantly better

Treatment Goal #4:

Significantly worse   Slightly worse   No change   Slightly better   Significantly better

Treatment Goal #5:

Significantly worse   Slightly worse   No change   Slightly better   Significantly better

Are there things that you did not achieve fully or that you still would like to continue to change and improve? If so, how could you make those changes?

_____

_____

_____

As I've said throughout the book, this treatment is not a static or final process. Rather, the treatment is designed to teach you a new way to approach your day-to-day activities. Hopefully, you have made many changes through the course of these chapters, and have many more changes in sight now that you've stopped avoiding and started living again. However, the changes in the future may be more associated with your new lifestyle without avoidance, rather than your life with it. For example, in a life without avoidance, a goal may be to learn to ice skate, to explore all of the state parks, or to finally take the dream vacation to Rome. Anything is possible when avoidance is no longer an obstacle.

WATCHING OUT FOR WARNING SIGNS

After plotting your symptoms and appreciating your changes (and your likely changes to come), you may notice that in certain weeks your negative emotions and avoidance came back. This is common during active treatment and not something to be hard on yourself about. However, before we end our work together, it is important for you learn how to prevent your symptoms from coming back. Although symptom return or relapse is uncommon after this treatment, it is possible given the right—or wrong—circumstances.

The most common reason for a return of symptoms (and avoidance) tends to be the experience of major life stressors. These stressors may be similar to what led you to start avoiding in the first place, as depicted in figure 1.1, Model for Negative Emotions. Whether it be a major illness, financial burden, or change in your social network (divorce, death of loved one, move, or retirement), these stressors can restart the cycle of negative emotions and avoidance.

There are some warning signs that precede the return of symptoms. The symptoms and types of avoidance shown in the table are common warning signs. It's a good idea to refresh your familiarity with them now, so you can recognize them quickly should they arise.

Negative Emotions	Avoidance
Anxiety	Situational Avoidance (stores, restaurants, highways)
Depression	Physical Avoidance (working out, walking stairs, swimming)
Fear	Thought Avoidance (talking about traumatic or painful memories)
Guilt	Positive Emotional Avoidance (social gatherings, hobbies, church, exercise)
Anger	Subtle Avoidance and Safety Behaviors (sitting off to the side, racing in and out of stores)

Another way to remain vigilant to the return of symptoms is to continue to periodically complete the Symptom Checklist that you used throughout this treatment and plotted earlier in this chapter. Please consider printing out a few copies and filling them out every six months, or whenever you notice any of the warning signs just listed. A good practice might be to schedule a time down the road to do a check-in using the monitoring form. Write a reminder by hand on a calendar if you use one, or use your phone to schedule it. Although the occasional use of avoidance is normal (for example, staying home to rest on Saturday after a long week at work), if the occasional avoidance becomes the norm, that should raise a flag of concern. Complete another Symptom Checklist and compare it to the Symptom Progression you plotted here and, if the warning signs are all there, review the previous chapters and exposure practices. In this way, you can take action to stop the avoidance before it has a chance to take over again. Additional copies of these forms can be printed from http://www.newharbinger.com/45663.

WRAPPING UP

This chapter focused on plotting your treatment progress at the symptom level as well as comparing your progress across your specified treatment goals. This highlighted how you've changed behaviorally (the video camera view) rather than how you feel (your score on the Symptom Checklist is unlikely to be zero = no symptoms). And we discussed how you can expect steady symptom improvements as you continue to practice and simply live with these new approaches to a life without avoidance. I cautioned you to continue to periodically monitor your symptoms with the checklist to watch out for warning signs that your symptoms are worsening. These checks are particularly important following significant stressors or changes in your life (say, prolonged illness or injury). I hope and expect that the skills you learned and practiced in this book have led you to significant positive changes in your life and that these changes will stick with you for years, if not decades, to come—because you have *stopped avoiding and started living*!

What to Do Next Along Your Journey

YOU MADE IT!

Now it is time to say goodbye. My hope is that you enjoyed this text and, far more importantly, that you found this book to be helpful. You should be able to better identify your negative emotions and your related avoidance and better understand the relation between the two. You also should know a lot about exposure and how you can use it to overcome your avoidance and improve your emotions, both the negative and the positive. While exposures may have sounded fairly straightforward at first, you learned how to apply them to different types of avoidance (situational, physical, thought, and positive emotions) as well as learning strategies for improving their effects by addressing interfering symptoms (negative thoughts, sleep disruption, alcohol use, and chronic pain). With a lot of hard work, you have come a long way to stop avoiding and start living again. And these are tools that should benefit you for years to come.

IF THIS TREATMENT WASN'T ENOUGH

I feel very strongly that this treatment will be successful for most people who try it and get all the way through to this point in the book. I have used it with hundreds of patients over the years and taught it to hundreds of providers to use with their own patients. I wish I could share all of the amazing success stories that I have heard over the years, but that would take several more books to cover. Instead, I was limited in sharing the stories of patients like Mark, Kelly, Earl, and Patricia. They were great patients, and I hope that you experienced similar gains. However, I also acknowledge that no one treatment will work for everyone. There are a lot of strengths in self-help treatments. They allow you to complete the treatment when you are ready and at your own pace, without making weekly drives to a therapist's office or paying weekly medical bills. However, at the same time, self-help treatments also have several limitations. No matter how interactive this text aimed to be, it cannot match the interaction that occurs with a real-life provider. And it is that piece that may lead you to seek additional treatment after completing this book. Based on your review of your treatment goals, seeking therapy (or psychiatric medications or adjustments of existing medications) may be the next step in your journey to overcome your negative emotions and related avoidance.

If you do elect to seek therapy going forward, I have a few pointers for you on how to pick a therapist. Assuming that my approach to treatment resonated with you, you should focus your search on providers of *evidence-based psychotherapies*, such as cognitive behavioral therapy (CBT). Evidence-based psychotherapies are structured, goal focused, and present oriented. They identify your problematic emotions, thoughts, and behaviors; set goals and targets for change; and work on changing the here and now to accomplish your goals. You'll need to be thoughtful and discerning in your search, as there are a lot of therapies and types of therapists out there. When selecting a therapist, look for one who advertises a similar approach to treatment, and consider bringing this book to session to review what worked well and what worked less well for you. This should give your therapist a good starting point to take you the remaining steps to stop avoiding and start living. However, if your therapist spends a lot of time asking about your childhood (focused on past processing), lets you talk more than they talk (supportive therapy), or emphasizes breathing and relaxation techniques more than behavioral or thought change (relaxation therapy), you should keep shopping.

Fortunately, there are a few online resources that may make your search for an evidence-based therapist easier. These resources are offered by organizations of psychologists dedicated to the science of psychology and evidence-based psychotherapy.

Association for Behavioral and Cognitive Therapies—Find a Therapist

http://www.findcbt.org/FAT/

Anxiety and Depression Association of America—Find a Therapist

https://members.adaa.org/search/custom.asp?id=4685

THANK YOU AND GOOD-BYE

Thank you for giving this text a chance. I hope that it was helpful in your journey toward a life filled with positive emotions (and diminished negative emotions and avoidance). If so, I encourage you to use what you've learned to help those around you through the same message to stop avoiding and start living. Whether it be through sharing this book or simply sharing the words of wisdom that you found to be most useful along your journey, helping others can be quite rewarding and result in positive emotions for both you and those you choose to help.

Symptom Tracking Form

Assessment	Date	Score
Treatment Assessments		
Time 1		
Time 2		
Time 3		
Time 4		
Time 5		
Time 6		
Follow-up Assessments		
6 months		
12 months		
18 months		
24 months		

Additional copies of this form can be printed from http://www.newharbinger.com/45663.

Scientific Evidence for Transdiagnostic Behavior Therapy

Bunnell, B. E., & Gros, D. F. (2017). Transdiagnostic behavior therapy (TBT) for generalized anxiety disorder. *International Journal of Case Studies, 6,* 1–8.

Gros, D. F. (2014). Development and initial evaluation of transdiagnostic behavior therapy (TBT) for veterans with affective disorders. *Psychiatry Research, 220,* 275–282.

Gros, D. F. (2015). Design challenges in transdiagnostic psychotherapy research: Comparing transdiagnostic behavior therapy (TBT) to existing evidence-based psychotherapy in veterans with affective disorders. *Contemporary Clinical Trials, 43,* 114–119.

Gros, D. F. (2019). Efficacy of transdiagnostic behavior therapy (TBT) across the affective disorders. *American Journal of Psychotherapy, 72,* 59–66.

Gros, D. F., & Allan, N. P. (2019). A randomized controlled trial comparing transdiagnostic behavior therapy (TBT) and behavioral activation in veterans with affective disorders. *Psychiatry Research, 281,* 112541.

Gros, D. F., Allan, N. P., & Szafranski, D. D. (2016). The movement towards transdiagnostic psychotherapeutic practices for the affective disorders. *Evidence Based Mental Health, 19,* e10–e12.

Gros, D. F., Merrifield, C., Hewitt, J., Elcock, A., Rowa, K., & McCabe, R. E. (2020). Preliminary findings for Group Transdiagnostic Behavior Therapy for affective disorders among youths. *American Journal of Psychotherapy.*

Gros, D. F., Merrifield, C. M., Rowa, K., Szafranski, D. D., Young, L., & McCabe, R. E. (2019). A naturalistic comparison of group transdiagnostic behavior therapy (TBT) and disorder-specific cognitive behavioral therapy groups for the affective disorders. *Behavioural and Cognitive Psychotherapy, 47,* 39–51.

Gros, D. F., & Oglesby, M. E. (2019). A new transdiagnostic psychotherapy for veterans with affective disorders: Transdiagnostic behavior therapy (TBT). *Psychiatry: Interpersonal and Biological Processes, 82,* 83–84.

Gros, D. F., Oglesby, M. E., & Allan, N. P. (2020). Efficacy of transdiagnostic behavior therapy (TBT) on transdiagnostic avoidance in veterans with emotional disorders. *Journal of Clinical Psychology, 76,* 31–39.

Gros, D. F., Szafranski, D. D., & Shead, S. D. (2017). A real world dissemination and implementation of transdiagnostic behavior therapy (TBT) for veterans with affective disorders. *Journal of Anxiety Disorders, 46,* 72–77.

Daniel F. Gros, PhD, is associate professor of psychiatry and behavioral sciences at the Medical University of South Carolina, and psychology program manager and research and development principal investigator at the Ralph H. Johnson VA Medical Center in Charleston, SC. He has published more than one hundred research articles, completed more than fifty conference presentations and workshops, and received more than $10 million in federal grant money to complete research for the VA and US Department of Defense on a number of topics, including transdiagnostic and evidence-based psychotherapies for individuals with depression, anxiety, and post-traumatic stress disorder (PTSD).

Real change *is* possible

For more than forty-five years, New Harbinger has published proven-effective self-help books and pioneering workbooks to help readers of all ages and backgrounds improve mental health and well-being, and achieve lasting personal growth. In addition, our spirituality books offer profound guidance for deepening awareness and cultivating healing, self-discovery, and fulfillment.

Founded by psychologist Matthew McKay and Patrick Fanning, New Harbinger is proud to be an independent, employee-owned company. Our books reflect our core values of integrity, innovation, commitment, sustainability, compassion, and trust. Written by leaders in the field and recommended by therapists worldwide, New Harbinger books are practical, accessible, and provide real tools for real change.

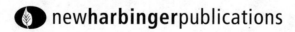 **newharbinger**publications

MORE BOOKS from
NEW HARBINGER PUBLICATIONS

THE ANXIETY & PHOBIA WORKBOOK, SEVENTH EDITION
978-1684034833 / US $25.95

ADULT CHILDREN OF EMOTIONALLY IMMATURE PARENTS
How to Heal from Distant, Rejecting, or Self-Involved Parents
978-1626251700 / US $18.95

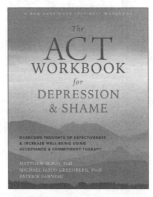

THE ACT WORKBOOK FOR DEPRESSION & SHAME
Overcome Thoughts of Defectiveness & Increase Well-Being Using Acceptance & Commitment Therapy
978-1684035540 / US $22.95

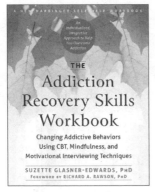

THE ADDICTION RECOVERY SKILLS WORKBOOK
Changing Addictive Behaviors Using CBT, Mindfulness & Motivational Interviewing Techniques
978-1626252783 / US $25.95

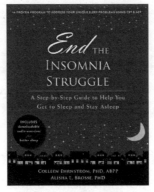

END THE INSOMNIA STRUGGLE
A Step-by-Step Guide to Help You Get to Sleep & Stay Asleep
978-1626253438 / US $24.95

THE DIALECTICAL BEHAVIOR THERAPY SKILLS WORKBOOK FOR PTSD
Practical Exercises for Overcoming Trauma & Post-Traumatic Stress Disorder
978-1684032648 / US $24.95

newharbingerpublications
1-800-748-6273 / newharbinger.com

(VISA, MC, AMEX / prices subject to change without notice)
Follow Us 📷 f 🐦 ▶ 📌 in

Don't miss out on new books in the subjects that interest you.
Sign up for our **Book Alerts** at **newharbinger.com/bookalerts**

Register your **new harbinger** titles for additional benefits!

When you register your **new harbinger** title—purchased in any format, from any source—you get access to benefits like the following:

- Downloadable accessories like printable worksheets and extra content

- Instructional videos and audio files

- Information about updates, corrections, and new editions

Not every title has accessories, but we're adding new material all the time.

Access free accessories in 3 easy steps:

1. Sign in at NewHarbinger.com (or **register** to create an account).

2. Click on **register a book**. Search for your title and click the **register** button when it appears.

3. Click on the **book cover or title** to go to its details page. Click on **accessories** to view and access files.

That's all there is to it!

If you need help, visit:

NewHarbinger.com/accessories

new harbinger
CELEBRATING
40 YEARS